NEW EDITION

STUDENT BOOK VOL.1

CHINESE GCSE (9-1)
中学汉语 （修订版）

主　编　李晓琪
副主编　罗青松

华语教学出版社·伦敦
Sinolingua · London

CHINESE GCSE (9-1) STUDENT BOOK VOL.1

Compiler-in-chief: Xiaoqi LI
Deputy compiler-in-chief: Qingsong LUO
Compilers: Xiaoyu LIU, Ya XUAN, Shuhong WANG

Advisers: Xiaoming ZHANG, Wei SHAO
Consultant editors: Wei SHAO, Hongxia DU, Jingjing ZHAO, Lu LIN

Editors: Shurong ZHAI, Ranran DU, Yang ZHANG
English proofreader: Rory Howard
Cover design: GEOMETRIC ORIGINAL ARTISTIC DESIGN Co., Ltd.
Layout/Illustrations: E°T创意工作室

Copyright © 2018 Sinolingua London Limited
First published in Great Britain in August 2018 by Sinolingua London Limited

Unit 13 Park Royal Metro Centre, Britannia Way
London, United Kingdom NW10 7PA
Tel: 0044(0)2089611919
Fax: 0044(0)2084530246
Email: editor@sinolingualondon.com

Printed in China 2018

ISBN 978-1-907838-48-4

编写说明

《中学汉语》是为以英语为母语的11-16岁中学生编写的汉语教材，全套教材分为三个等级（第一册、第二册和第三册）九本书，每个等级包括学生用书（课本）、教师用书和练习册。全套教材还配有汉语词语卡片、MP3朗读光盘、PowerPoint课件和网上资源等多媒体产品。每册教材可使用一学年（参考学时为90-100学时），全套教材可以供三个年级使用。

一、设计框架

《中学汉语》采用了以2017年新版GCSE Chinese (9-1)大纲中的交际话题为主线，以语言项目为核心，以文化内容为基本要素的综合性构架，力求做到设计理念与时俱进，语言知识扎实科学，文化内涵丰富生动。

1. 以话题为主线

教材每册有八个单元，每个单元由相关话题的三篇课文组成。每册教材都基本涵盖了2017年Edexcel, AQA新版GCSE Chinese大纲的主要话题的相关内容，并参照了Asset Language的语言学习要求。教材围绕话题主线，针对不同等级，在语言形式、文化内容上逐步拓展丰富。这种编排方式使学习者无论选取任何阶段的教材，都可较全面地接触新版GCSE Chinese大纲的交际话题，从而在提高交际能力，以及准备考试方面得到帮助。如：初学者可以在学完第一、二册后，参加GCSE Chinese考试，第三册则用于巩固提高，并逐步向AS/A-Level级别过渡。而具备一定汉语基础的学生，也可以直接从第二册或第三册开始学习。

2. 以语言项目为核心

教材以新版GCSE Chinese大纲提供的560个核心词语和85个语法项目为教材内容的重点与核心，全套教材覆盖了新大纲的全部语言项目——词汇和语言点。此外，还根据日常交际需要，以及教学对象、学习环境的特点，进行了合理调整与拓展，以达到在控制教材难度的基础上，丰富教材内容，满足话题表达需求的目的。教材各等级语言项目分布如下：

第一册：汉字145个左右，生词237个，句型91个。

第二册：汉字150个左右，生词233个，句型93个。

第三册：汉字160个左右，生词230个，句型95个。

书中句型除了在新版大纲基础上进行拓展之外，编写组还从教材语言点设置与编排的科学性与实用性出发，将新版大纲中概括表述的句型具体化，并进行合理分级。如在新版GCSE Chinese大纲中，情态动词只作为一个语言点给出，用"他会说普通话"概括这一语言形式，我们在教材中处理为"他能说普通话"、"你应该学习中文"等多个语言点。这样不仅更全面地表现出情态动词的特点，也便于在教学中分解难点，科学、合理、有序、全面地安排教学内容。

3. 以文化内容为基本要素

《中学汉语》注重文化内容，并将其与语言学习目标、教学对象与教学环境结合起来加以体现。本套教材的文化内容反映在话题设计、课文内容、练习设计、画面提示、教学提示等方面，以期逐步培养学习者的目的文化意识，拓展他们的文化视野；而通过教材丰富多样的文化体现，也可进一步增强教材的知识性与趣味性。

二、教材结构

1. 学生用书

学生用书是教材的核心。每课的基本版块有学习目标提示、课文、词语、语法点讲解、学习小贴士以及模仿考试题型所设置的听说读写译练习。学生用书上的练习作为课堂操练使用，主要围绕教学目标，从听说读写译几个方面进行操练。每三课为一个单元，每个单元后有句型小结，帮助学生总结语言知识；同时，还设置了与单元话题相关的文化常识，以增进学生对中国文化、现代生活、社会国情的认识和了解。学生用书的编写原则是简明、适用，符合课堂教学需要，同时又注重效果，循序渐进地增进学生的语言技能与文化认知。

2. 教师用书

教师用书的主要作用是帮助教师较为便捷地在内容、方法上进行教学准备。每课的基本版块有：教学内容提示、教学步骤与建议、练习参考答案、相关语言知识点和文化背景知识的简要说明，此外，还根据教学需要，提供了一些课堂活动和小游戏。每个单元提供了一套单元测验题，考题设计综合了单元学习内容，形式上也逐步靠近GCSE Chinese考试题型。教师在教学中可用于考查学生阶段学习情况，从而循序渐进地帮助学生适应考试，最终达到GCSE Chinese考试的标准。

3. 练习册

练习册为教材提供外围的辅助练习，练习安排与学生用书中的练习相辅相成，作为课堂练习的拓展，供学习者课下使用，或用来丰富课堂训练项目。提供多样化的练习，可以进一步充实课堂教学的内容；提供有选择的练习，也可以让学生有机会自主学习，增强自学能力。

4. 其他配套资源

为方便使用者，本套教材还有生词卡片、多媒体材料等，增加教与学的互动性和生动性，方便师生课堂教学和自学。

三、教材特色

《中学汉语》关注教学对象的特点，注重使用者的基本目的和要求，教材的突出特点表现为以下几个方面。

1．针对性与目的性统一

本套教材针对中学阶段的英语为母语的汉语学习者编写。通过本套教材的学习，学生可全面提高汉语交际能力，并在听说读写技能上全面达到GCSE Chinese考试大纲的标准和要求。

2．全面性与基础性统一

本套教材在话题、语音、汉字、词汇、句型、文化等方面，全面覆盖新版GCSE Chinese考试大纲的内容；同时，根据学生水平等级、交际需要及汉语本身的特点进行全面规划，合理增补，科学编排。同时，教材设计也充分考虑到中学生汉语学习的基本目标与认知特点，突出基础知识、基本技能的掌握，注重内容编排难度、容量、梯级的合理性。

3．科学性与趣味性统一

教材针对教学对象的特点，体现寓教于乐的编写理念。话题贴近学生现实生活，生活场景的设置真实自然，课文内容自然活泼，练习形式丰富多样，注重实用性和互动性。此外，教材还通过图文并茂的文化介绍，拓展学生文化视野，增强教材的趣味性，从而使得学习者获得有趣、有用的汉语学习体验。

为此套教材的策划和出版，华语教学出版社的王君校社长、韩晖总编和常青图书公司的茹静总经理，以及华教社伦敦分社的责任编辑翟淑蓉、杜然然付出了大量的心血，对此我们表示衷心的感谢；此外英国指导团队的张小明、杜宏霞、赵晶晶、林璐老师和梁乔、邵炜、何晓红、吴允红、黄珍理等诸位一线教师的积极参与，为本教材的问世给予了很大的帮助，我们编写组的全体成员对你们也说一声：谢谢！

设计一套全面系统的针对性教材，是一项有挑战性的工作，需要长期努力。我们的错误和疏漏在所难免，期望各位同仁提出宝贵意见，我们将不断完善，使《中学汉语》更好地为课堂教学提供帮助。

《中学汉语》编写组

Compilers' Words

Chinese GCSE is designed for secondary school students in English speaking countries aged 11-16. This three-volume series covers three levels. Each level includes a student's book, a workbook, a teacher's book, Chinese character flash cards, MP3 audio CD, and multimedia support through PowerPoint courseware and online resources. Each volume corresponds to one academic year (90-100 class hours) and the whole series can be used consecutively over three grades.

Design Framework

Chinese GCSE is organised according to the 2017 new GCSE Chinese specification with a topic-oriented structure that takes the language as its core, and cultural contents as its key elements. The series is thus designed as a full set of materials, which includes both comprehensive language knowledge and enriched cultural content.

1. Key Topics

The series covers all the areas in the 2017 new Edexcel GCSE Chinese and AQA syllabus, and takes the Asset Language requirements as its reference. Each volume has eight units, with each unit containing three lessons that focus on one topic or activity. The vocabulary and grammar develop step by step so that students may familiarise themselves with the new topics involved in the new GCSE Chinese syllabus, while simultaneously developing their conversational skills as they prepare for the exam. Beginners may take the GCSE exam after completing the first two volumes, and then take the third volume as a preparatory guide for the AS/A-Level exam. Those who have a certain command of the Chinese language may start from either volume 2 or 3.

2. Language as the Core

The series covers all the 560 core words and 85 grammar points required by the new GCSE Chinese syllabus. On top of this, the contents have been organized and extended in a manner which will satisfy the daily communicative needs of the learners, while also ensuring the inclusion of extensive content and expressions, all of which are based on the GCSE Chinese course requirements. The language points are arranged as follows:

Volume 1: 145 Chinese characters, 237 new words, 91 sentence patterns

Volume 2: 150 Chinese characters, 233 new words, 93 sentence patterns

Volume 3: 160 Chinese characters, 230 new words, 95 sentence patterns

The sentence patterns have been extended based on the new GCSE Chinese syllabus, and they have been substantiated and sequenced according to their level of difficulty. For example, in the new GCSE Chinese syllabus, the modal verb is given as a language point and expressed in the sentence 他会说普通话. However, in this series we have modified that entry into several language points, such as 他能说普通话, 你应该学习中文, etc. This more fully displays the characteristics of modal verbs, helps to ease learning difficulties, and provides a better organization and format of instruction.

3. Cultural Content a the Key Element

Chinese GCSE places an emphasis on cultural content, which is combined with language objectives and methods of teaching to provide a nurturing learning environment. As shown in the topics, texts, exercises, screen highlights and teaching tips of the series, the cultural content is aimed at cultivating students' cultural consciousness and extending their cultural vision. This diversified cultural content renders the books more interesting and informative to students, which in turn makes it a more effective learning tool.

Structure of the Series

1. Student's Book

The Student's Book is the core book of the series. Each lesson consists of sections such as learning objectives, text, new words, grammar points, learning tips and relevant exam exercises for listening, speaking, reading, writing and translating. The exercises in the Student's Book can be used in class for practice. Three lessons form a unit, followed by a unit summary which reviews the language points of the lessons, and also includes cultural tips that emphasise contemporary Chinese society, utilise real-life situations and modern scenarios for a more comprehensive understanding of Chinese. The Student's Book is both concise and practical, and aims to develop the language learning skills and cultural recognition of the students in a gradual manner.

2. Teacher's Book

The Teacher's Book prepares the instructors to teach the series' content in a fun and nurturing learning environment. Each lesson includes teaching suggestions, keys to the exercises, and additional cultural information. Furthermore, the Teacher's Book provides a number of suggestions for classroom activities and games. A test is provided after each unit based on its contents, and is close to the GCSE test in format. This test can serve as a tool to gauge the students' progress and further prepare them for the GCSE exams.

3. Exercise Book

This includes exercises as a complement to the Student's Book. As an extension of classroom exercises, it may be used both in class and at home. These varieties of exercises not only supplement classroom teaching, but also provide materials for self study and a chance for the students to improve their language abilities outside of class.

4. Additional Resources

The series also provides illustrations of commonly used words, flash cards, and multimedia software to further increase the convenience of teaching and self study, which makes both the teaching and studying of this series a more interactive and dynamic process.

Features

This series has been closely tailored to meet the students' basic objectives and studying needs. This has been done through the following:

1. Having an Aligned Focus

The target readers of the series are secondary school Chinese language students whose native language is English. Through their study, students can fully improve their communicative ability in Chinese and reach the standard required to successfully sit the GCSE Chinese exam in listening, speaking, and reading and writing.

2. Fully Integrating the Basic Language Knowledge

This series covers all the requirements of the new GCSE Chinese syllabus in its topics, phonetics, characters, vocabularies, sentences, cultural knowledge etc. It is clearly organized into different levels of language ability and knowledge, various social settings and the characteristics of the Chinese language and culture. The objectives and recognition patterns of secondary school students have been fully taken into consideration. The series emphasises a command of language knowledge and skills, as well as more difficult and advanced language points to encourage further study.

3. Being Practical and Fun to Use

The topics covered relate to the students' lives and include realistic scenarios; the contents are very dynamic, and the exercises are diverse, practical and useful. Through illustrated cultural introductions, the series expands the cultural visions of the students and creates a more interesting learning environment. As a result of this, we hope the students will in turn have a rewarding experience learning Chinese.

For the help and support during the compilation of this series, we would like to extend our heartfelt thanks to Mr. Wang Junxiao, President of Sinolingua, Ms. Han Hui, Editor-in-chief of Sinolingua, Ms. Rujing, Managing Director of Cypress Books, as well as editors Zhai Shurong and Du Ranran from Sinolingua London Ltd. Thanks also go to the advisor team, Zhang Xiaoming, Du Hongxia, Zhao Jingjing, Lin Lu as well as many other frontline teachers, such as Liang Qiao, Shao Wei, He Xiaohong, Wu Yunhong, Huang Zhenli in Britain.

It is a challenge to compile a series of textbooks that is both comprehensive and practical, and with a clear academic focus. We have thoroughly enjoyed this process of creation, and we welcome the opinions and comments of our peers and students.

Characters in the Text

大海 Dàhǎi
中国人 Chinese

小雨 Xiǎoyǔ
中国人 Chinese

天天 Tiāntiān
中国人 Chinese

京京 Jīngjīng
中国人 Chinese

Characters in the Text

大卫 Dàwèi David
英国人　British

玛丽 Mǎlì Mary
英国人　British

本 Běn Ben
英国人　British

丽丽 Lìli Lily
英国人　British

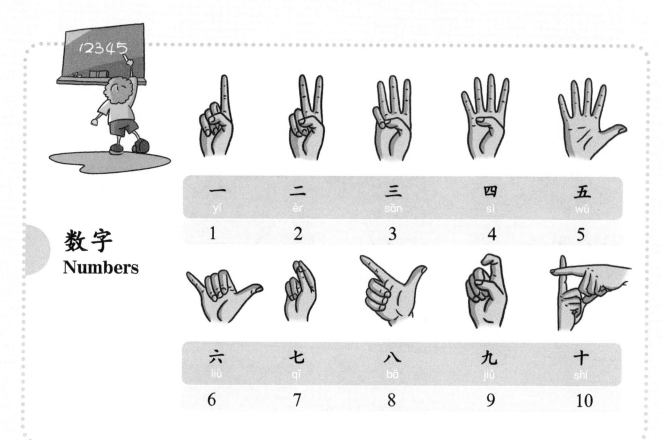

数字
Numbers

一	二	三	四	五
yī	èr	sān	sì	wǔ
1	2	3	4	5

六	七	八	九	十
liù	qī	bā	jiǔ	shí
6	7	8	9	10

缩略语
Abbreviations

n.	noun	名词
v.	verb	动词
adj.	adjective	形容词
num.	numeral	数词
m.w.	measure word	量词
pron.	pronoun	代词
adv.	adverb	副词
prep.	preposition	介词
conj.	conjunction	连词
part.	particle	助词
int.	interjection	叹词

社交用语
Social Greetings

Hello.	你好。
Hello, everyone.	大家好。
Good evening.	晚上好。
Good night.	晚安。
Goodbye.	再见。
See you tomorrow.	明天见。
Excuse me.	请问。
Thank you.	谢谢。
Sorry.	对不起。
It doesn't matter.	没关系。

课堂用语
Classroom Expressions

Good morning.	早上好。
Hello, Miss/Sir.	老师好。
Hello, everyone.	同学们好。
It's time for class.	现在上课。
Read after me.	跟我读。
Once again please.	再说一遍。
Time for break.	休息一会儿。
Class is over.	现在下课。

目 录
CONTENTS

Unit 5 活动与爱好 Activities and Hobbies

Unit 6 外出与交通 Travel and Transport

Unit 7 影视与音乐 TV, Movies and Music

Unit 8 理想与计划 Ideals and Plans

词汇表 Vocabulary

第一课 Lesson

Hello 你好 **1**

Learning Objectives

交际话题 Topic of conversation:
问好 Greetings
Wèn hǎo

基本句型 Sentence patterns:
你好。
你好吗?
我很好。

你好。

你好。

New Words

1. 好 hǎo **adj.** good, fine
2. 很 hěn **adv.** very
3. 吗 ma **part.** used for 'Yes/No' questions
4. 我 wǒ **pron.** I, me
5. 你 nǐ **pron.** you (singular)
6. 您 nín **pron.** the respectful form of 你 (singular)
7. 一 yī **num.** one
8. 二 èr **num.** two
9. 三 sān **num.** three
10. 四 sì **num.** four
11. 五 wǔ **num.** five

Text

大卫： 你好。
Dàwèi: Nǐ hǎo.

玛丽： 你好。
Mǎlì: Nǐ hǎo.

David: Hello.
Mary: Hello.

大卫： 您好。
Dàwèi: Nín hǎo.

老师： 你好。
Lǎoshī: Nǐ hǎo.

David: Hello.
Teacher: Hello.

天天： 你好吗?
Tiāntiān: Nǐ hǎo ma?

小雨： 我很好。
Xiǎoyǔ: Wǒ hěn hǎo.

Tiantian: How are you?
Xiaoyu: I'm fine.

Grammar Point

1. 吗 is a modal particle. If you want to ask a 'yes/no' question, all you need to do is to put 吗 at the end of a statement. The word order follows exactly that of the declarative sentence.
e.g. 你好吗? 我很好。

2. We have learned that 很 means 'very', however, please note that you must use 很 in the following example whether or not you are saying the word 'very'. Therefore, it is incorrect to just reply "我好"。
e.g. 我很好。(√) 我好。(×)

Exercises

Listen 1 Number the following items in the order that they are played in the recording.

I	you	good	very	you (respectful form)

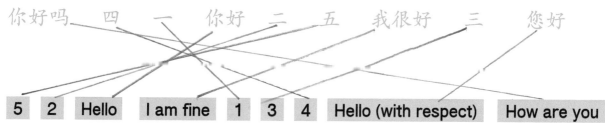

三　　　　　一　　　　　二　　　　　五　　　　　四

Read 2 Link the pinyin with the Chinese.

Nǐ hǎo.　　　　Nín hǎo.　　　　Nǐ hǎo ma?　　　　Wǒ hěn hǎo.

你好吗?　　　　我很好。　　　　你好。　　　　您好。

Read 3 Link the characters with the English.

你好吗　四　一　你好　二　五　我很好　三　您好

5　2　Hello　I am fine　1　3　4　Hello (with respect)　How are you

Write 4 Translate the following sentences into English.

1）你好。 Hello

2）您好。 Hello (respect)

3）你好吗? How are you?

4）我很好。 I am fine

Speak 5 Try different greetings in Chinese with your classmates.

1）A: Hello.

　　B: Hi.

2）A: How are you?

　　B: I'm fine.

Write 6 Complete the sentences with appropriate Chinese characters.

1）你 好。　　　2）您 好。　　　3）我 很好。

Write 7 Practise Chinese characters.

数字 Numbers

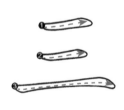

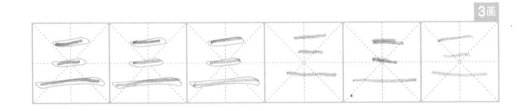

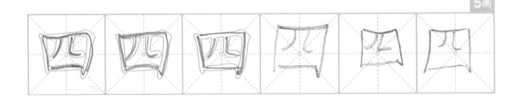

第二课 Lesson **2**

What's Your Name? 你叫什么？

Learning Objectives

交际话题 Topic of conversation:

名字和国籍 Names and Nationalities
Míngzi hé guójí

基本句型 Sentence patterns:

你叫什么？　　我叫玛丽。
你是英国人吗？　我是中国人。他不是中国人。

New Words

1 叫 jiào v. to call
2 什么 shénme pron. what
3 是 shì v. to be (e.g. am; is; are)
4 不 bù adv. not
5 英国 Yīngguó n. UK, Britain
6 中国 Zhōngguó n. China
7 法国 Fǎguó n. France
8 美国 Měiguó n. USA
9 亚洲 Yàzhōu n. Asia

10 欧洲 Ōuzhōu n. Europe
11 美洲 Měizhōu n. America
12 人 rén n. people
13 他 tā pron. he, him
14 六 liù num. six
15 七 qī num. seven
16 八 bā num. eight
17 九 jiǔ num. nine
18 十 shí num. ten

Text

Part I

大卫： 你好， 我叫大卫。 你叫什么?
Dàwèi : Nǐ hǎo, wǒ jiào Dàwèi. Nǐ jiào shénme?

玛丽： 我叫玛丽。
Mǎlì : Wǒ jiào Mǎlì.

David: Hello. My name is David.
What is your name?
Mary:　My name is Mary.

Brain Teaser

Look at the following questions. How is the Chinese sentence order different from English?
你是英国人吗? 你叫什么?

大卫： 你是英国人吗?
Dàwèi : Nǐ shì Yīngguórén ma ?

小雨： 我不是英国人，
Xiǎoyǔ : Wǒ bú shì Yīngguórén,

　　　　 我是中国人。
　　　　 wǒ shì Zhōngguórén.

大卫： 他是中国人吗?
Dàwèi : Tā shì Zhōngguórén ma?

小雨： 他不是中国人， 他是法国人。
Xiǎoyǔ : Tā bú shì Zhōngguórén , tā shì Fǎguórén.

Learning Tip

Talking about nationality is simple. This is how it works:
Name of the country + 人 = citizens of the country
e.g. 中国－中国人； 英国－英国人；美国－美国人。

David: Are you British?
Xiaoyu: I'm not British, I'm Chinese.
David: Is he Chinese?
Xiaoyu: He is not Chinese. He is French.

Grammar Point

1.什么 means 'what'. It is used in 'open' questions (where the answer is not 'yes/no'). It is not always at the beginning of a sentence like in English. Instead, 什么 is in the same place as where the answer will be.
e.g. 你叫什么?
　　 我叫玛丽。

2.是 means 'am, are, is'. In Chinese, verbs do not change as much as they do in English. 是 also stays in the same place in questions, unlike questions in English (You are.../Are you...?)
e.g. 我是中国人。
　　 他是中国人。
　　 你是中国人吗?

3.不是 means 'is not'. In English, negative words go after verbs. In Chinese it is the opposite!
e.g. 我不是中国人。

Part II

我叫大卫
Wǒ jiào Dàwèi

我叫大卫，是英国人，是欧洲人。他叫小欧，是法国人，是欧洲人。
Wǒ jiào Dàwèi, shì Yīngguórén, shì Ōuzhōurén. Tā jiào Xiǎo'ōu, shì Fǎguórén, shì Ōuzhōurén.

他叫天天，是中国人，是亚洲人。本是美国人，他不是欧洲人，不是
Tā jiào Tiāntiān, shì Zhōngguórén, shì Yàzhōu rén. Běn shì Měiguórén, tā bú shì Ōuzhōu rén, bú shì

亚洲人，他是美洲人。
Yàzhōurén, tā shì Měizhōurén.

Exercises

Listen 1 Number the following items in the order that they are played in the recording.

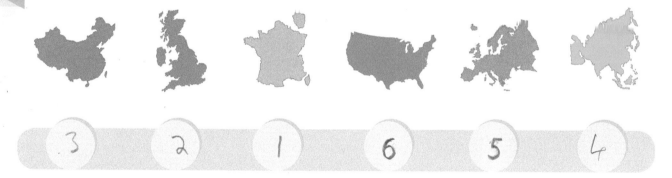

3 2 1 6 5 4

Listen 2 Listen to the recording and put a cross (X) in the correct boxes.

	英国	法国	中国	美国	亚洲	欧洲
Dongdong			X			
Meimei						
Yingying						
Xiaolu						
Xiaoyan						
Dashan						
Dalin						

Read
3 Read part II of the text and fill in the blanks with David (大卫), Ben (本), Xiao Ou (小欧), Tiantian (天天). You can use each person more than once.

1) __天天__ is Chinese.

2) __本__ is American.

3) __大卫__ is British.

4) __小欧__ is French.

5) __大卫__ and __小欧__ are European.

6) __天天__ is Asian.

7) __本__ is not Asian or European.

Read
4 Link the English with the Chinese.

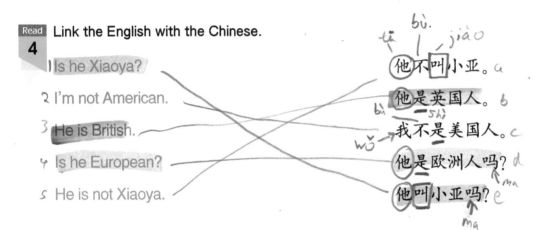

1 Is he Xiaoya?

2 I'm not American.

3 He is British.

4 Is he European?

5 He is not Xiaoya.

他不叫小亚。a

他是英国人。b

我不是美国人。c

他是欧洲人吗？d

他叫小亚吗？e

Write
5 Translate the following sentences into English.

1) 我是英国人。 *I am British*

2) 我不是中国人。 *I am not Chinese*

3) 他是法国人。 *He is French*

4) 你是欧洲人吗? *Are you European?*

Speak
6 Talk about the people below in Chinese. What is your name and where are you from?

e.g. 你好。我叫Mike，我是美国人。

Mike

小美

Mingming

Lisa

Speak 7 Role play. Ask your partner 'yes/no' questions about the characters in exercise 6.

> **e.g.** 小美是中国人吗？ — 是，她是中国人。
>
> Mike是英国人吗？ — 不是，Mike是美国人。

Write 8 Complete the sentences with appropriate Chinese characters.

1) 你好，我 ☐ 大卫。你叫 ☐ ☐ ？

2) 您 ☐ 英国人 ☐ ？

3) 他 ☐ 是美国 ☐ ，他是法国 ☐ 。

Write 9 Practise Chinese characters.

 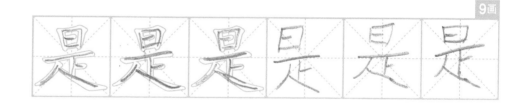

 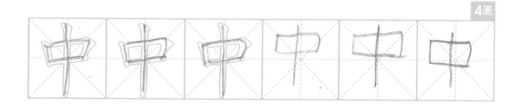

 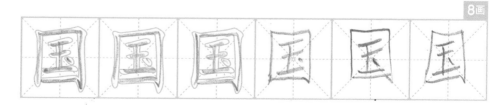

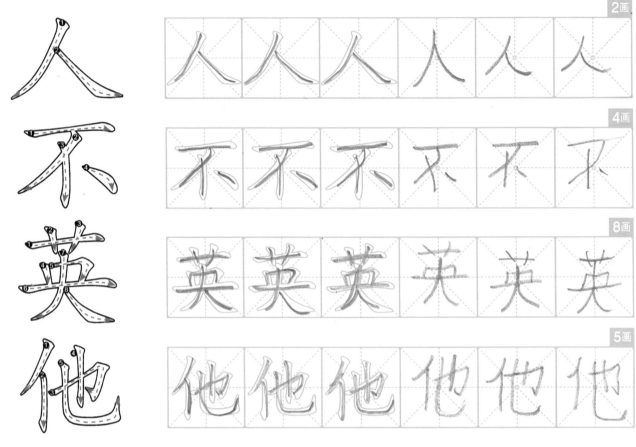

数字 Numbers

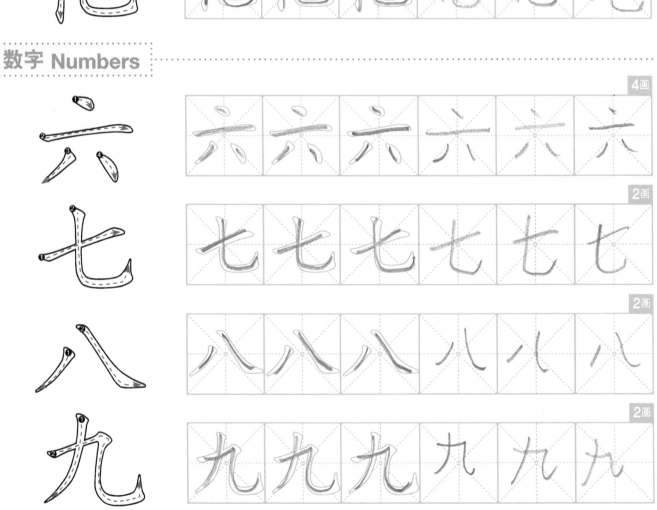

第三课 Lesson

3

Where Do You Live? 你家在哪儿?

Learning Objectives

交际话题 Topic of conversation:

居住地　Place of Residence
Jūzhùdì

基本句型 Sentence patterns:

他在哪儿?　　你家在哪儿?　　我家在北京。

你家在哪儿?

我家在北京。

New Words

1 她 tā **pron.** she, her
2 北京 Běijīng **n.** Beijing
3 上海 Shànghǎi **n.** Shanghai
4 香港 Xiānggǎng **n.** Hong Kong
5 台湾 Táiwān **n.** Taiwan
6 伦敦 Lúndūn **n.** London
7 家 jiā **n.** home, family
8 在 zài **v.** to be in, to be at
9 哪儿 nǎr **pron.** where

Text

Part I

大卫： 你好，我叫大卫，他叫本。你叫什么？
Dàwèi：　Nǐ hǎo，　wǒ jiào Dàwèi，　　tā jiào Běn.　Nǐ jiào shénme?

小雨： 我叫小雨。
Xiǎoyǔ：　Wǒ jiào Xiǎoyǔ.

大卫： 你是英国人吗？
Dàwèi：　Nǐ shì Yīngguórén ma?

小雨： 我不是英国人，我是中国人。
Xiǎoyǔ：　Wǒ bú shì Yīngguórén，　wǒ shì Zhōngguórén.

大卫： 你家在哪儿？
Dàwèi：　Nǐ jiā zài nǎr?

小雨： 我家在北京。你家在哪儿？
Xiǎoyǔ：　Wǒ jiā zài Běijīng.　Nǐ jiā zài nǎr?

大卫： 我家在伦敦。
Dàwèi：　Wǒ jiā zài Lúndūn.

David: Hello. My name is David, he is Ben.
　　　　What's your name?
Xiaoyu: My name is Xiaoyu.
David: Are you British?
Xiaoyu: I'm not British. I'm Chinese.
David: Where do you live?
Xiaoyu: I live in Beijing. Where do you live?
David: I live in London.

Learning Tip

In this lesson, we learn the character 她 'she'. Although it sounds the same as 他 'he', it is a completely different character! You will come across more characters that sound the same but have different written forms and meanings. In English, these are called 'homonyms'. Can you think of any homonyms in English?

大卫： 她叫什么？
Dàwèi： Tā jiào shénme?

丽丽： 她叫京京。
Lìli： Tā jiào Jīngjīng.

大卫： 她是英国人吗？
Dàwèi： Tā shì Yīngguórén ma?

丽丽： 她不是英国人，
Lìli： Tā bú shì Yīngguórén,

  她是中国人。
  tā shì Zhōngguórén.

大卫： 她在哪儿？
Dàwèi： Tā zài nǎr?

丽丽： 她在香港。
Lìli： Tā zài Xiānggǎng.

David: What's her name?
Lily: She is Jingjing.
David: Is she British?
Lily: She is not British, she is Chinese.
David: Where is she?
Lily: She is in Hong Kong.

Grammar Point

1. 在 means 'to be at, to be in', therefore, there is no need to add 是 'to be' in front of 在.
   e.g. 她在香港。(√)
       她是在香港。(×)

2. 哪儿 usually means 'where'. It can be used in 'open' questions. Be aware of its position – it is not always at the beginning of a question like in English. Instead, 哪儿 is in the same place in the sentence as where the answer will be.
   e.g. 我家在哪儿？我家在北京。

Part II

我家在上海
Wǒ jiā zài Shànghǎi

我叫天天，我是中国人，我家在上海。她叫小英，她家在台湾。
Wǒ jiàoTiāntiān, wǒ shì Zhōngguórén, wǒ jiā zài Shànghǎi. Tā jiào Xiǎoyīng, tā jiā zài Táiwān.

她叫小雨，她家不在香港，她家在北京。
Tā jiào Xiǎoyǔ. tā jiā bú zài Xiānggǎng, tā jiā zài Běijīng.

Exercises

Listen 1 Number the following items in the order that they are played in the recording.

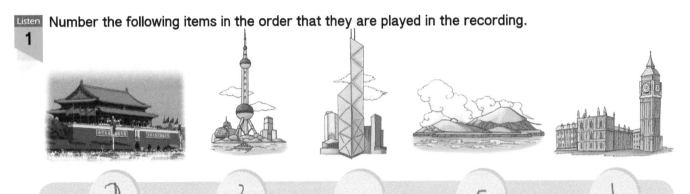

2   3   4   5   1

Listen 2 Listen to the recording and put a cross (X) in the correct boxes.

	北京	台湾	香港	上海	伦敦
Mary				X	
Xiaoying		X			
David					X
Xiaonan	X				
Youyou			X		

(handwritten above headers: beijing, taiwan, hong kong, Shanghai, London)

Read 3 Read part II of the text and complete the gaps in each sentence using a word from the box below. There are more words than gaps.

British   Taiwan   American   Shanghai   London   Chinese   French

1) Xiaoyu's home is in ___Beijing___ .

2) Xiaoying's home is in ___Taiwan___ .

3) Tiantian's home is in ___Shanghai___ , he is ___Chinese___ .

Read 4 Link the English with the Chinese.

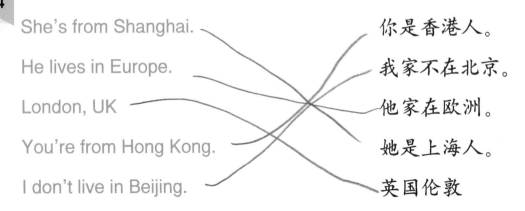

She's from Shanghai.   你是香港人。

He lives in Europe.   我家不在北京。

London, UK   他家在欧洲。

You're from Hong Kong.   她是上海人。

I don't live in Beijing.   英国伦敦

Read 5 Read the sentence and match it with picture A or B.

B

他家在台湾。

B

我家不在伦敦，在美国。

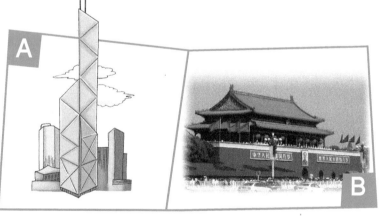

B

她是北京人。

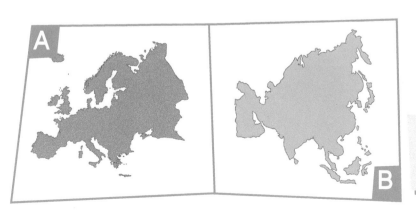

B

你是亚洲人。

上海很好。

Write 6 Translate the following sentences into English.

1）她家在哪儿？ ....

2）你是上海人吗？ ....

3）我家在中国北京。 ....

4）他是英国人，家在伦敦。 ....

5）我不是北京人，我是香港人。 ....

Speak 7 Talk about the pictures below in Chinese, describe their nationalities and where their homes are.

e.g. 大卫是英国人，他家在伦敦。

大卫

小雨

大海

小英

Speak
8 Role play. Tell your partner where you are from and where your home is.

e.g. 我是中国人，我家在北京。

Write
9 Complete the sentences with appropriate Chinese characters.

1）我叫小英，我 [ ] 台湾人。

2）我家 [ ] 香港，香港很好。

3）[ ] 叫小欧，他是法国人，他 [ ] 在欧洲。

4）你是中国人 [ ] ？你家在 [ ] [ ] ？

Write
10

Practise Chinese characters.

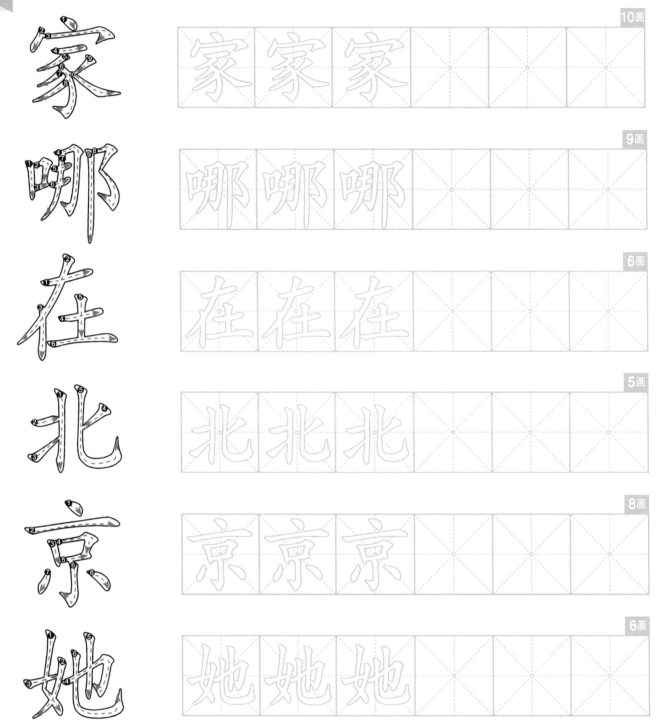

文化常识 Cultural Tip

Chinese name

When it comes to names, Chinese people have their own traditions and their names have special characteristics. Unlike Westerners, Chinese people put their family name first and then their given name. Given names usually have one or two Chinese characters. Because some Chinese names sound similar or are very popular, new-born babies can now have given names of three characters to avoid confusion.

Chinese names are meant to convey a special meaning. Given names often express hope for the new-born. For example, names such as 忠 (faithful) and 义 (righteous) embody virtues that parents hope their child

will have. While names like 康 (health) and 富 (happiness) express wishes for life. Some other given names imply birthplace or time of birth, for example 京 (Beijing) and 晨 (morning).

第一单元小结　　Unit One　Summary

Greetings

你好／您好。Hello.	**您** is more polite and shows respect
你好吗？How are you? 我很好。I am fine.	Statement + 吗？(Yes/No question)

Numbers 1-10

一，二，三，四，五，六，七，八，九，十

Talking about names

你叫什么？What is your name? 她叫什么？What is her name?	Someone + 叫 + 什么？
我叫玛丽。My name is Mary. 她叫小英。Her name is Xiaoying.	Someone + 叫 + name.

Talking about nationalities

我是中国人。I am Chinese. 他是伦敦人。He is from London.	Someone + 是 + country/area + 人
她不是中国人。She is not Chinese. 他不是伦敦人。He is not from London.	Someone + 不 + 是 + country/area + 人
你是中国人吗？Are you Chinese? 他是伦敦人吗？Is he from London?	Someone + 是 + country/area + 人 + 吗？

Talking about locations

你在哪儿？Where are you?	Someone + 在 + 哪儿？
我在台湾。I am in Taiwan.	Someone + 在 + location
你家在哪儿？Where is your home?	Someone + 家 + 在 + 哪儿？
我家在北京。 My home is in Beijing.	Someone + 家 + 在 + location

第四课 Lesson

This Is My Father 这是我爸爸 4

Learning Objectives

交际话题 Topic of conversation:

家庭成员　Family Members
Jiātíng chéngyuán

基本句型 Sentence patterns:

你家有几口人？我家有五口人。
这是我爸爸。　那是我妈妈。　这是你哥哥吗？

New Words

1. 这 zhè　pron. this
2. 那 nà　pron. that
3. 爸爸 bàba　n. father
4. 妈妈 māma　n. mother
5. 哥哥 gēge　n. elder brother
6. 姐姐 jiějie　n. elder sister
7. 弟弟 dìdi　n. younger brother
8. 口 kǒu　m.w. measure word used when addressing the entire number of people in a family
   n. mouth
9. 有 yǒu　v. to have (indicates ownership or existence)
10. 几 jǐ　pron. how many
11. 妹妹 mèimei　n. younger sister
12. 和 hé　conj. and

Text

Part I

大卫： 你好。
Dàwèi： Nǐ hǎo.

小雨： 你好。
Xiǎoyǔ： Nǐ hǎo.

大卫： 你叫什么？
Dàwèi： Nǐ jiào shénme？

小雨： 我叫小雨。
Xiǎoyǔ： Wǒ jiào Xiǎoyǔ.

这是我姐姐，
Zhè shì wǒ jiějie,

她叫小美。
tā jiào Xiǎoměi.

David: Hello.
Xiaoyu: Hello.
David: What's your name?
Xiaoyu: My name is Xiaoyu. This is my elder sister. Her name is Xiaomei.

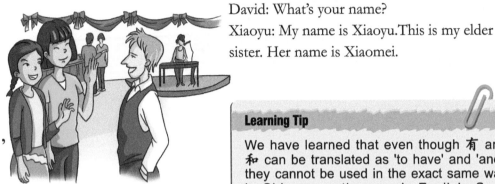

Learning Tip

We have learned that even though 有 and 和 can be translated as 'to have' and 'and', they cannot be used in the exact same way in Chinese as they are in English. Such mismatches between Chinese and English make learning a new language challenging.

Dahai: How many people are there in your family?
Jingjing: There are five people in my family, my mum, my dad, my elder brother, my little brother and me.
Dahai: This is my father. That is my mother.
Jingjing: Is this your elder brother?
Dahai: Yes. This is my elder brother. That is my younger brother.

大海： 你家有几口人？
Dàhǎi： Nǐ jiā yǒu jǐ kǒu rén？

京京： 我家有五口人，我妈妈，
Jīngjīng： Wǒ jiā yǒu wǔ kǒu rén, wǒ māma,

我爸爸，我哥哥，我弟弟和我。
wǒ bàba, wǒ gēge, wǒ dìdi hé wǒ.

大海： 这是我爸爸，那是我妈妈。
Dàhǎi： Zhè shì wǒ bàba. nà shì wǒ māma.

京京： 这是你哥哥吗？
Jīngjīng： Zhè shì nǐ gēge ma？

大海： 是，这是我哥哥，那是我弟弟。
Dàhǎi： Shì, zhè shì wǒ gēge, nà shì wǒ dìdi.

Grammar Point

1. 有 means 'to have'. It can be used to express existence. When used to show existence, 有 is similar to saying 'there is' or 'there are' in English.
e.g. 你家有几口人？ 我家有三口人。

2. Measure words are used with numbers to indicate the quantity of a noun. The general term for 'measure word' in linguistics is 'classifier' because they classify the amount or number of a noun. Measure words are more common in Chinese than English. Use the following pattern: Number + measure word + noun.
e.g. 五口人。
三个人。
gè
四只猫。
zhī

3. 几 is usually used to ask about numbers less than ten. In a question, 几 is always in the same place as where the answer will be.
e.g. 你家有几口人？
我家有五口人。

4. 和 can ONLY be used to connect single items (one noun to another noun). It CANNOT connect one sentence to another. Use the following pattern:
Noun 1 (something/someone) + 和 + noun 2 (something/someone)
e.g. 我家有三口人，爸爸、妈妈和我。

Part II

这是我爸爸
Zhè shì wǒ bàba

我叫天天， 我是中国人。这是我家， 我家在中国上海。我家有五
Wǒ jiào Tiāntiān,　wǒ shì Zhōngguórén. Zhè shì wǒ jiā,　wǒ jiā zài Zhōngguó Shǎnghǎi. wǒ jiā yǒu wǔ

口人。这是我爸爸， 那是我妈妈， 这是我， 那是我弟弟和我妹妹。
kǒu rén.　Zhè shì wǒ bàba,　nà shì wǒ māma,　zhè shì wǒ,　nà shì wǒ dìdi hé wǒ mèimei.

Exercises

Listen 1 Number the following items in the order that they are played in the recording.

Listen 2 Listen to the recording and fill in the blanks with English.

1）This is my ....　　4）That is his ....

2）That is my ....　　5）She is not my ....

3）This is his ....　　6）Is she your .... ?

Read 3 Read part II of the text and answer the following questions in English.

1) Where is Tiantian from?

....

2) Where is Tiantian's home?

....

3) How many people are there in Tiantian's family and who are they?

....

Read 4 Link the pinyin with the Chinese.

zhè	姐姐
nà	哥哥
bàba	那
māma	妈妈
gēge	这
jiějie	弟弟
dìdi	和
mèimei	爸爸
hé	妹妹

Read 5 Read the sentence and match it with picture A or B.

A

B

这是我哥哥。

那是我妈妈。

那是我哥哥和姐姐。

这是我妈妈和妹妹。

Write 6 Translate the following sentences into English.

1）这是大海家。...

2）这是他爸爸和妈妈。...

3）那是他妹妹。...

4）这是他。...

5）那不是他哥哥。..

Speak
7 Talk about the pictures in Chinese.

e.g. 我家有四口人。这是我妈妈，那是我弟弟。

Write
8 Complete the sentences with appropriate Chinese characters.

1）□ 是我家。

2）这是我爸爸，□ 是我妈妈。

3）这是 □ 哥哥吗？

4）那是我姐姐 □ 弟弟。

5）她 □ 是我姐姐，她是我妹妹。

Write
9 Practise Chinese characters.

第五课 Lesson

5

His House Is Not Big 他家不大

Learning Objectives

交际话题 Topic of conversation:

家 House
Jiā

基本句型 Sentence patterns:

他家不大。他家有四个房间。我没有小狗。我有一只猫。

New Words

1. 个 gè **m.w.** (a measure word)
2. 房间 fángjiān **n.** room
3. 大 dà **adj.** big
4. 小 xiǎo **adj.** small, little
5. 没 méi **adv.** not, no
6. 两 liǎng **num.** two (before measure word)
7. 只 zhī **m.w.** (a measure word for certain animals, e.g. cat, dog, bird, etc.)
8. 猫 māo **n.** cat
9. 狗 gǒu **n.** dog

Text

Part I

玛丽： 这是 本家吗？
Mǎlì： Zhè shì Běn jiā ma ?

大卫： 是。
Dàwèi： Shì.

玛丽： 他家大吗？
Mǎlì： Tā jiā dà ma ?

大卫： 他家不大， 他家有四个房间。
Dàwèi： Tā jiā bú dà, tā jiā yǒu sì gè fángjiān.

Learning Tip

A lot of nouns have specific measure words assigned to them. For example, 只 is used for relatively small animals. You will come across many new measure words which are used with specific nouns in the future.

Mary: Is this Ben's house?

David: Yes.

Mary: Is his house big?

David: His house is not big. There are four rooms in his house.

大卫： 你有 小狗 吗？
Dàwèi： Nǐ yǒu xiǎo gǒu ma ?

玛丽： 我没有小狗， 我有一只小猫。
Mǎlì： Wǒ méiyǒu xiǎo gǒu, wǒ yǒu yì zhī xiǎo māo.

你家有 狗 吗？
Nǐ jiā yǒu gǒu ma ?

大卫： 有， 我家有 两只小狗。
Dàwèi： Yǒu, wǒ jiā yǒu liǎng zhī xiǎo gǒu.

David: Do you have puppies?

Mary: No, I don't have puppies. I have a kitten.
Do you have dogs?

David: Yes. I have two puppies in my house.

Grammar Point

1. 个 is one of the most common measure words. It can be used with nouns that do not have specific measure words.
e.g. 一个房间。两个哥哥。

2. 很 and 不 are useful for describing a topic (a noun or a person). You can put both of these characters before adjectives. Both 很 and 不 can all stress a great degree. Be aware, the verb 是 'am, is, are' is not used in this pattern.
Topic + 很/不 + adjective (description/comment)
e.g. 他家不大。弟弟很小 。

Part II

我的家
Wǒ de jiā

我叫大卫，我是英国人。我家在英国伦敦。我家不大，有四个
Wǒ jiào Dàwèi,　wǒ shì Yīnguórén.　Wǒ jiā zài Yīngguó Lúndūn.　Wǒ jiā bú dà,　yǒu sì gè

房间。我有一个弟弟和一个妹妹。妹妹有一只小猫，我有一只小狗。
fángjiān.　Wǒ yǒu yí gè　dìdi　hé yí gè mèimei.　Mèimei yǒu yì zhī xiǎo māo,　wǒ yǒu yì zhī xiǎo gǒu.

弟弟很小，他没有猫和狗。
Dìdi　hěn xiǎo,　tā méiyǒu māo hé gǒu.

Exercises

Listen 1 Number the following items in the order that they are played in the recording.

Listen 2 Listen to the recording and put a cross (X) in the correct boxes.

	Xiaoyu	Xiaolong	Lanlan	Junjun	Jingjing

Read 3 Read part II of the text and put a cross in the correct box.

1) David is ....

☐	French
☐	British
☐	Chinese
☐	American

2) David has .... siblings.

☐	2
☐	3
☐	4
☐	5

3) David's house has .... rooms.

☐	2
☐	3
☐	4
☐	5

4) David has ....

☐	1 dog
☐	2 dogs
☐	1 cat
☐	2 cats

Read 4 Link the pinyin with the Chinese.

méi   liǎng   zhī   gè   gǒu   yǒu   xiǎo   fángjiān   māo   dà

有   个   房间   大   小   没   两   只   猫   狗

Read 5 Read the sentence and match it with picture A or B.

四个房间

五只猫

六只狗

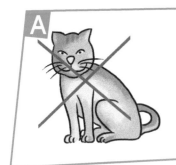

没有猫

三个哥哥

两个妹妹

Write 6 Translate the following sentences into English.

1）我家很大。

2）她家有五个房间。

3）他有两个姐姐。

4）我没有弟弟。

5）我有三只小狗。

Speak 7 Talk about the pictures in Chinese.

Speak 8 Role play. Describe your home to your partner in Chinese, then let him or her translate what you said back into English.

> **e.g.** 我家有四口人，我爸爸，我妈妈……
>
> 我家不大。
>
> 我家有三个房间。
>
> 我有一只狗。

Write 9 Complete the sentences with appropriate Chinese characters.

1）他家不大，他家很 ⬜ 。　　2）我家 ⬜ 三个房间。

3）我 ⬜ 有猫，我有狗。　　4）她有一 ⬜ 姐姐。

5）她家有两 ⬜ 狗。

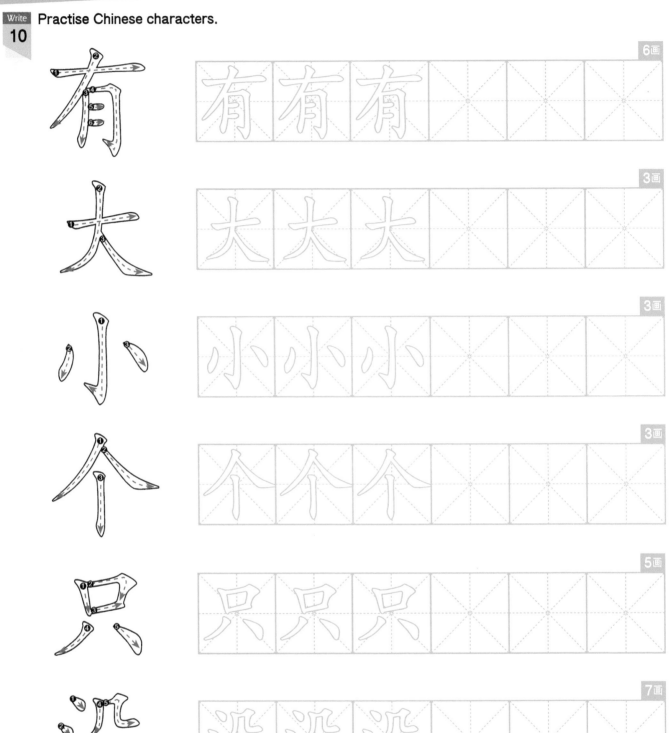

Write 10 Practise Chinese characters.

第六课 Lesson

He Is My Friend 他是我的朋友

6

Learning Objectives

交际话题 Topic of conversation:

我的朋友 My Friend
Wǒ de péngyou

基本句型 Sentence patterns:

他是谁？　他是我的朋友。
她是中学生。

New Words

1 谁 shuí/shéi **pron.** who

2 朋友 péngyou **n.** friend

3 老师 lǎoshī **n.** teacher

4 同学 tóngxué **n.** classmate

5 中学生 zhōngxuéshēng **n.** middle school student

6 的 de **part.** (a structural particle)

7 爷爷 yéye **n.** grandfather

8 奶奶 nǎinai **n.** grandmother

Text

Part I

玛丽：　他是谁?
Mǎlì:　　Tā shì shuí ?

大卫：　他是我的朋友，叫本。
Dàwèi:　Tā shì wǒ de péngyou, jiào Běn.

玛丽：　他家在美国吗?
Mǎlì:　　Tā jiā zài Měiguó ma ?

大卫：　他家不在美国，在英国。
Dàwèi:　Tā jiā bú zài Měiguó, zài Yīngguó.

Mary: Who is he?

David: He is my friend, Ben.

Mary: Is he living in the USA?

David: No, his home is not in the USA. He lives in Britain.

大海：　这是我的老师。
Dàhǎi:　Zhè shì wǒ de lǎoshī.

京京：　老师，您好! 我叫京京。
Jīngjīng:　Lǎoshī, nín hǎo ! Wǒ jiào Jīngjīng.

大海：　这是我的同学。
Dàhǎi:　Zhè shì wǒ de tóngxué.

老师：　你好，京京，你是北京人吗?
lǎoshī:　Nǐ hǎo, Jīngjīng, nǐ shì Běijīngrén ma ?

京京：　我不是北京人，我是香港人。
Jīngjīng:　Wǒ bú shì Běijīngrén, wǒ shì Xiānggǎngrén.

Dahai: This is my teacher.

Jingjing: Hello, teacher! My name is Jingjing.

Dahai: This is my classmate.

Teacher: Hello, Jingjing. Is Beijing your hometown?

Jingjing: No, it's not. My hometown is Hong Kong.

Learning Tip:

What are the open questions words we have learned so far and how are they used differently in Chinese?
For example: 你叫什么? 你家在哪儿? 他家有几口人? 她是谁?

Grammar Point

1. The character 的 is a modification of nouns. It can be used to form the meaning of possessiveness and belonging. However, It can be omitted when use in front of the family or family member.
   e.g. 我的; 他的; 谁的
   　　 我家; 我爸爸; 我妹妹

2. 谁 is another question word used in 'open' questions. In a question, 谁 is always in the same place as where the answer will be.
   e.g. 他是谁?
   　　 他是我的朋友。

她是中学生
Tā shì Zhōngxuéshēng

这是我的好朋友 小英，她是 中学生。她是亚洲人，她家在台湾。
Zhè shì wǒ de hǎo péngyou Xiǎoyīng, tā shì zhōngxuéshēng. Tā shì Yàzhōurén, tā jiā zài Táiwān.

小英的家很大，有六个房间。小英和爸爸、妈妈、弟弟、妹妹在台湾。
Xiǎoyīng de jiā hěn dà, yǒu liù gè fángjiān. Xiǎoyīng hé bàba, māma, dìdi, mèimei zài Táiwān.

她家有 两只小猫。她的爷爷和奶奶在欧洲，他们有一只大狗。
Tā jiā yǒu liǎng zhī xiǎo māo. Tā de yéye hé nǎinai zài Ōuzhōu, tāmen yǒu yì zhī dà gǒu.

Exercises

Listen 1 Number the following items in the order that they are played in the recording.

Listen 2 Listen to the recording and put a cross (X) in the correct boxes.

	朋友	中学生	老师	同学
Xiaoyu and Lanlan				
Dahai and I				
Xiaoming				
Jingjing				

Read 3 Read part II of the text and complete the gaps in each sentence using a word from the box below. There are more words than gaps.

Britain   Hong Kong   America   London   Europe   Taiwan   father   mother   younger

brother   younger sister   grandfather   grandmother   nine   six   four   one   two   three

1) Xiaoying's home is in . . . .

2) Xiaoying's home has . . . . rooms.

3) Xiaoying's . . . . and . . . . are in Europe.

4) Xiaoying has . . . . cat(s).

Read 4 Link the pinyin with the Chinese.

de   lǎoshī   tóngxué   yéye   nǎinai   péngyou   shuí   zhōngxuéshēng

谁   爷爷   老师   朋友   同学   奶奶   中学生   的

Read 5 Read the sentence and match it with picture A or B.

我的老师

她的朋友

爷爷和奶奶

一个中学生

没有朋友

两个老师

Write 6 Translate the following sentences into English.

1）她是一个好老师。 ....

2）小狗是我的好朋友。 ....

3）谁家有小猫？ ....

4）她姐姐是中学生。 ....

5）这是我的同学。 ....

Speak 7 Talk about the pictures in Chinese, describe their professions and where their homes are.

e.g. 杰克是老师，他是美国人，他家住在美国。

Speak 8 Role play. Bring a photo of you and your friends. Tell your partner who they are and what their professions (e.g. students) are.

e.g. 这是我的朋友David，他是中学生。

Write 9 Complete the sentences with appropriate Chinese characters.

1) 我是一个中 ☐ ☐ 。

2) 他是 ☐ ？是你的同学吗？

3) 大卫是我的好 ☐ ☐ 。 ☐ 是他的狗。

4) 你的老师是中国人吗？不，我的 ☐ ☐ 是英国人。

5) 这是我 ☐ 狗，那是大卫 ☐ 狗。

Write 10 Practise Chinese characters.

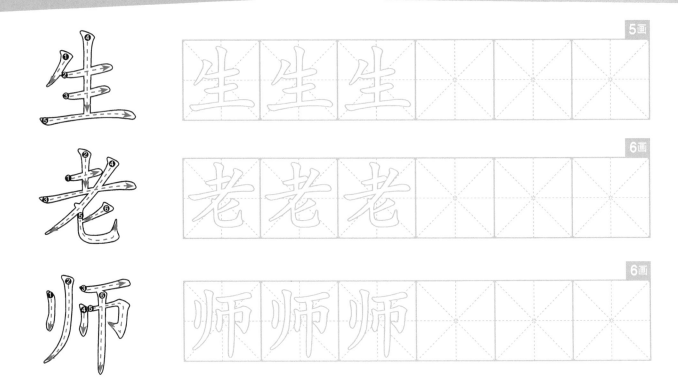

5画 生 生 生

6画 老 老 老

6画 师 师 师

文化常识 Cultural Tip

The Chinese Family

China is a society in which family is highly valued. 'Family harmony is the basis for success in any undertaking' is a saying that Chinese people believe in. The parent-child relationship is an important part of Chinese culture. Parents bring up their children and work hard all their lives for them. They also look after their children's children, namely, their grandchildren.

Western family relationships are more independent. Parents have fewer responsibilities when their children have reached adulthood. This may be why

the parent-child relationship in western countries is not as intimate as that in China. In China, children are raised by their parents and parents are supported by their children when they get old; such traditional family relations come from the thinking of the wise and virtuous philosopher, Confucius. His beliefs, including on the importance of family, are a central part of Chinese thinking.

Source from: *When in China-A Guide to Chinese Business Culture*

第二单元小结　Unit Two Summary

Talking about my family

你家有几口人？ How many people are there in your family? 我家有四口人。 There are four people in my family.	你家＋ 有 ＋几＋口人？ 我家＋ 有 ＋number＋口人。
这是你爸爸吗？　Is this your dad? 那是她妈妈吗？　Is that her mum?	这/那 ＋ 是 ＋ someone ＋ 吗？
这不是我爸爸。This is not my dad. 那不是她妈妈。That is not her mum.	这/那 ＋ (不)是 ＋ someone。

Describing a topic (topic + comment)

我家不大。My house is not big. 他家很大。His house is big.	Topic ＋ 很/不 ＋ adjective (description/comment)

Talking about existence and ownership

他家有四个房间。 There are four rooms in his house. 我有两个妹妹。 I have two younger sisters. 我有一只小猫。I have a kitten.	Somewhere/someone ＋ 有 ＋ number ＋ measure word ＋ noun (something/ someone)
我没有狗。I don't have dogs. 他家没有四个房间。 There aren't four rooms in his house.	Somewhere/someone ＋ 没有 ＋ number ＋ measure word ＋ noun

Talking about possession

我 I - 我的 my 你 you - 你的 your 他 he - 他的 his 她 she – 她的 her 大卫 David – 大卫的 David's	Someone ＋ 的

第二单元小结　Unit Two Summary	
Talking about identities and jobs	
他是谁？Who is he?	Someone + 是 + 谁?
他是我的朋友。He is my friend. 他是学生。He is a student.	Someone + 是 + identity/profession
Measure words	
个 The most widely used measure word. It can be used with many objectives that do not have specific measure words.	一个房间 one room 两个人 two people
只 Used for relatively small animals.	五只猫 five cats 九只狗 nine dogs

第七课 Lesson

7

Everyone Drinks Tea 每个人都喝茶

Learning Objectives

交际话题 Topic of conversation:

饮食 Food and Drinks
Yǐnshí

基本句型 Sentence patterns:

早上好！　　他喝茶。
他不喝咖啡。 每个人都喝茶。

New Words

1 早上 zǎoshang　n. morning
2 吃 chī　v. to eat
3 喝 hē　v. to drink
4 茶 chá　n. tea
5 咖啡 kāfēi　n. coffee
6 水 shuǐ　n. water
7 牛奶 niúnǎi　n. milk

8 面包 miànbāo　n. bread
9 鸡蛋 jīdàn　n. egg
10 每 měi　pron. every
11 都 dōu　adv. both, all
12 饭 fàn　n. meal
13 早饭 zǎofàn　n. breakfast

Text

Part I

妈妈： 早上 好，京京。
Māma:　Zǎoshang hǎo, Jīngjīng.

京京： 早上 好，妈妈。
Jīngjīng: Zǎoshang hǎo,　māma.

妈妈： 你吃什么？
Māma:　Nǐ chī shénme?

京京： 我吃面包。
Jīngjīng: Wǒ chī miànbāo.

妈妈： 你喝什么？
Māma:　Nǐ hē shénme?

京京： 我不喝牛奶，我喝茶，
Jīngjīng: Wǒ bù hē niúnǎi.　wǒ hē chá,

您喝什么？
nín hē shénme?

妈妈： 我喝茶。
Māma:　Wǒ hē chá.

京京： 爸爸喝咖啡吗？
Jīngjīng:　Bàba hē kāfēi ma?

妈妈： 爸爸不喝咖啡，
Māma:　Bàba bù hē kāfēi,

他喝茶。
tā hē chá.

京京： 每个人都喝茶。
Jīngjīng:　Měi gè rén dōu hē chá.

Mum: Good morning, Jingjing.

Jingjing: Good morning, mum.

Mum: What would you like to eat?

Jingjing: I will eat bread.

Mum: What would you like to drink?

Jingjing: I don't drink milk, I will drink tea.
　　　　How about you?

Mum: I will drink tea.

Jingjing: Does dad drink coffee?

Mum: Dad doesn't drink coffee,
　　　he drinks tea.

Jingjing: Everyone drinks tea.

Brain Teaser

Look at the following questions.
How is the Chinese sentence
order different from English?
你吃什么？ 你喝什么？
我吃面包。 我喝茶。

Learning Tip

We have already learned that 口 means 'mouth'. Can you
spot 口 in the characters 吃，喝，咖啡? Some characters
can be used to form a part of other characters in Chinese.
Remember these characters can help you learn related
characters more easily. The parts of a character can
sometimes help you guess the meaning of other characters
as well.

Grammar Point

1. 都 is often used to sum up the preceding
elements.e.g. 爸爸和妈妈都喝茶。

2. Where you see 每 (every), you will usually find 都
later in the sentence. Use the following pattern:
每 + measure word + noun + 都 …
e.g. 每个人都喝咖啡。
每个人都吃早饭。

Part II

四十七 **47**

每个人都喝茶

这是我家的早饭。我吃面包，喝茶。哥哥吃鸡蛋，喝茶，他不喝水。妈妈喝茶，喝牛奶。爸爸喝茶，他不喝咖啡。每个人都喝茶。

Exercises

Listen 1 Number the following items in the order that they are played in the recording.

Listen 2 Listen to the recording and put a cross (X) in the correct boxes.

	tea	milk	bread	egg	coffee	breakfast	water
this						X	
father							
mother							
elder sister							
I							
kitten							
elder brother							

Read 3 Read the sentences and match them with the correct pictures.

妈妈喝咖啡。	姐姐喝水。	哥哥吃鸡蛋。
爸爸吃面包。	我不喝牛奶。	我们都喝茶。

Read 4 Read the following paragraph and answer the questions below in English.

　　这是姐姐的早饭，她喝果汁，吃面包；那是哥哥的早饭，哥哥不喝果汁，他喝水，吃面包。每个人都吃面包。

Questions:

1）Whose breakfast is this?

2）What does elder sister drink for breakfast?

3）Whose breakfast is that?

4）What does elder brother eat for breakfast?

Speak
5

Talk about the pictures in Chinese.

	妈妈喝什么？	爸爸喝什么？	姐姐喝什么？	哥哥喝什么？	我喝什么？	小猫喝什么？
牛奶						
咖啡	✕					
茶						
水						

e.g. 我家有四口人。这是我妈妈，那是我弟弟。

Speak
6

Role play. Tell your partner about your family and what each member has for breakfast.

e.g. 我家有四口人……　　　这是我家的早饭。我吃……；我喝……；

我妈妈吃……，我爸爸喝……

Write 7 Complete the sentences with appropriate Chinese characters.

1）京京，早 ⬚ 好！

2）这是爸爸的 ⬚ 饭。

3）妈妈早饭吃面包，不 ⬚ 鸡蛋。

4）姐姐喝 ⬚ 奶，她不喝茶。

Write 8 Translate the following sentences into English.

1）我喝茶。

2）哥哥不喝咖啡。

3）每个人都喝茶。

4）我们都吃面包。

Write 9 Translate the following sentences into Chinese.

1）Good morning.

2）My name is David.

3）Everyone drinks tea.

4）**My mum doesn't eat egg.**

Write
10 Practise Chinese characters.

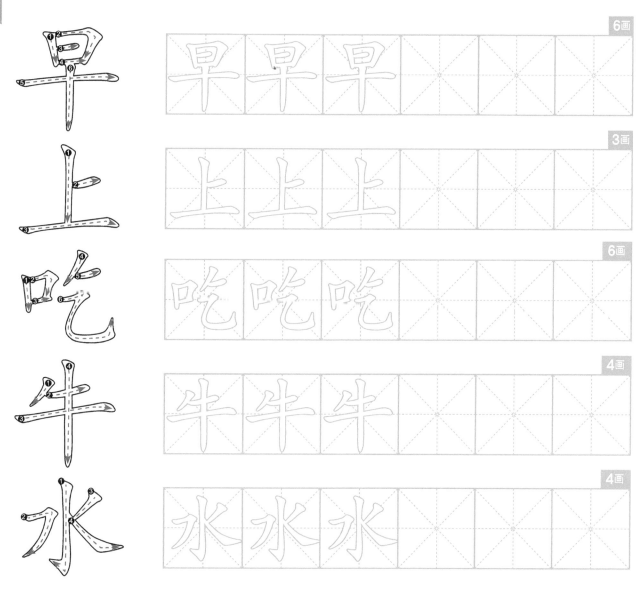

第八课　Lesson

8

The Red Apple Is Big! 这个红苹果很大！

Learning Objectives

交际话题 Topic of conversation:

蔬菜和饮料　Vegetables and Drinks
shūcài hé yǐnliào

基本句型 Sentence patterns:

你要水果吗？　　我要苹果，你呢？
这个红苹果很大。　我要绿色的蔬菜。
我要喝粉红色的汽水。

New Words

1　苹果 píngguǒ　n. apple
2　红(色) hóng (sè)　adj. red
3　要 yào　v. to want
4　水果 shuǐguǒ　n. fruit
5　呢 ne　part. (interrogative word)
6　果汁 guǒzhī　n. juice
7　汽水 qìshuǐ　n. soft drink
8　绿(色) lǜ (sè)　adj. green
9　粉红(色) fěnhóng (sè)　adj. pink
10　蔬菜 shūcài　n. vegetable
11　今天 jīntiān　n. today
12　黄(色) huáng(sè)　adj. yellow

Text

Part I

（在超市）
Zài chāoshì

天天： 你要水果吗？
Tiāntiān： Nǐ yào shuǐguǒ ma？

小雨： 我要苹果，你呢？
Xiǎoyǔ： Wǒ yào píngguǒ， nǐ ne？

天天： 我要汽水。
Tiāntiān： Wǒ yào qìshuǐ。

小雨： 这个红苹果很大，我要这个。
Xiǎoyǔ： Zhège hóng píngguǒ hěn dà， wǒ yào zhège。

天天： 我要那个汽水，粉红色的。
Tiāntiān： Wǒ yào nàge qìshuǐ， fěnhóngsè de。

(In the supermarket)
Tiantian: Do you want some fruit?
Xiaoyu: I want an apple. How about you?
Tiantian: I want a soft drink.
Xiaoyu: This red apple is big.
I want this one.
Tiantian: I want that soft drink,
the pink one.

Learning Tip

When you use a time phrase to describe an action (a verb), the time phrase must be used in front of the verb, or at the beginning of the sentence.
e.g. 你今天吃什么？ 今天你吃什么？

（在餐厅）
Zài cāntīng

天天： 小雨，今天你吃什么？
Tiāntiān： Xiǎoyǔ， jīntiān nǐ chī shénme？

小雨： 我要吃绿色的蔬菜，你呢？
Xiǎoyǔ： Wǒ yào chī lùsè de shūcài， nǐ ne？

天天： 我要水果，黄色的苹果。
Tiāntiān： Wǒ yào shuǐguǒ， huángsè de píngguǒ。

你喝什么？
Nǐ hē shénme？

小雨： 我喝果汁。
Xiǎoyǔ： Wǒ hē guǒzhī。

(In the restaurant)

Tiantian: What would you like to have today, Xiaoyu?

Xiaoyu: I would like green vegetables.How about you?

Tiantian: I want fruit, a yellow apple. What would you like to drink?

Xiaoyu: I'll drink juice.

Grammar Point

1.The particle 呢 can be used to ask reciprocal questions, or 'bounce back' questions. For example, 你呢 can be translated as 'and you?' or 'how about you?'.
e.g. 我要苹果，你呢？我很好。你呢？

2.Here are more examples of the 'Topic + comment' pattern, which can used to describe things. Use the following pattern:
Topic (something/someone) +很/不 + adjective (description/comment)

e.g. 这个红苹果很大。
    那只猫很小。
    我的家不大。

3. We know that 的 can indicate possessive meanings. Another very common function of 的 is to spice up boring nouns with sassy adjectives! Use the following pattern:
Adjective + 的 + noun (something/someone)
e.g. 绿色的青菜
    红色的苹果

Part II

这个红苹果很大

今天早饭，我吃面包和蔬菜，喝果汁，不喝茶。姐姐吃水果，她今天吃苹果，这个红苹果很大。哥哥喝咖啡，不喝牛奶。妈妈喝茶，她吃蔬菜，绿色的蔬菜。爸爸吃面包，喝汽水，喝粉红色的汽水。

Exercises

Listen 1 Number the following items in the order that they are played in the recording.

Listen 2 Listen to the recording and put a cross (X) in the correct boxes.

	bread	egg	vegetable	apple	juice	water	soft drink	tea	coffee
I	X				X				
elder sister									
elder brother									
mother									
father									

Read 3 Read the sentences and match them with the correct pictures.

 A

 B

 C

 D

 E

 F

哥哥喝果汁。

妈妈吃蔬菜。

粉红色的水果。

小雨要汽水。

这个红苹果很大。

绿色的汽水。

Read
4

Read the following text and put a cross in the correct box.

这是老师的早饭，她吃蔬菜和水果，她喝茶和果汁。那是我的早饭，我要面包、鸡蛋和水果。我的红苹果很大。我喝汽水和果汁，我不喝茶。

1) The teacher has .... and .... for breakfast.

☐ egg	☐ bread	☐ vegetable	☐ soft drink	☐ fruit

2) I do not drink ....

☐ juice	☐ tea
☐ soft drink	☐ coffee

3) The colour of my apple is ....

☐ yellow	☐ green
☐ red	☐ not mentioned

Speak
5

Talk about the pictures in Chinese.

	小美吃什么？	小雨喝什么？	玛丽喝什么？	大卫吃什么？	本吃什么？
黄色的水果	✕				
苹果					
汽水					
粉红色的水果					
蔬菜					

e.g. 小美吃什么？　小美吃苹果。

Speak
6
Role play. Below are the things you can order from a coffee shop. Play 'waiter/waitress and customer' with your partner. Be sure to say the colour of the item when placing your order.

红色的苹果　　绿色的苹果　　红色的果汁　　绿色的果汁　　黄色的果汁　　粉红色的果汁

红色的汽水　　绿色的汽水　　黄色的汽水　　粉红色的汽水　　黄色的蔬菜　　绿色的蔬菜

e.g. 你吃什么？　我吃绿色的苹果。

你喝什么？　我喝红色的果汁和黄色的汽水。

Write
7
Complete the sentences with appropriate Chinese characters.

1) 小英，你喝果 ☐ 吗？

2) 我要红色的苹 ☐ 。

3) 姐姐要果汁，不 ☐ 汽水。

4) 妈妈的早餐是绿 ☐ 的蔬菜。

5) 哥哥喝 ☐ 水，他不喝牛奶。

6) 你喝什么？我喝咖啡，你 ☐ ？

7) 今 ☐ 你吃什么？

8) 粉红色 ☐ 果汁。

Write 8 Translate the following sentences into English.

1）你要水果吗？ ....

2）我要苹果，你呢？ ....

3）这个黄苹果很大。 ....

4）这是我的绿色蔬菜。 ....

Write 9 Translate the following sentences into Chinese.

1） She is Chinese.

....

2） I live in London.

....

3） My younger sister drinks milk.

....

4） The red apple is big.

....

Write 10 Practise Chinese characters.

8画

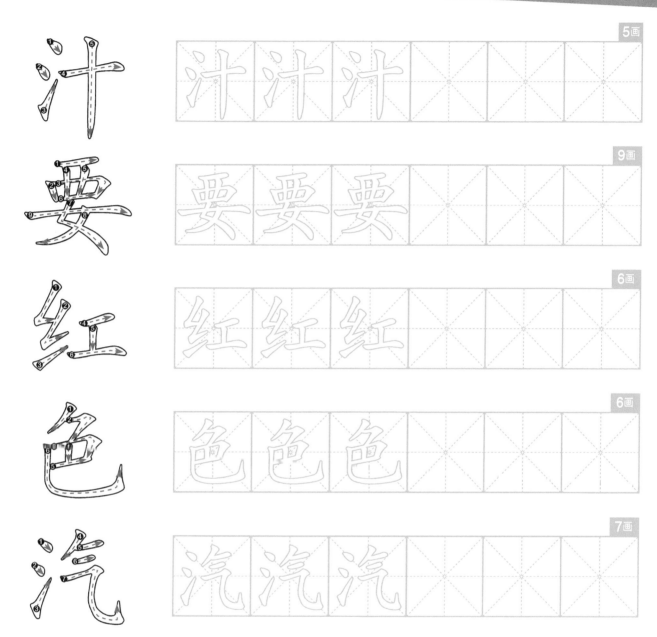

第九课 Lesson **9**

He Likes Chinese Noodles 他喜欢吃中国面条

Learning Objectives

交际话题 Topic of conversation:

饮食喜好　Food and Drink Preferences
Yǐnshí　xǐhào

基本句型 Sentence patterns:

你喜欢海鲜吗？　我喜欢牛肉，本也喜欢牛肉。

你喜欢吃鱼吗？　她喜欢海鲜，也喜欢青菜。

New Words

1. 喜欢 xǐhuan　v. to like
2. 海鲜 hǎixiān　n. seafood
3. 青菜 qīngcài　n. green vegetable
4. 牛肉 niúròu　n. beef
5. 鱼 yú　n. fish
6. 也 yě　adv. also, too
7. 米饭 mǐfàn　n. rice
8. 面条 miàntiáo　n. noodles
9. 谢谢 xièxie　v. thank you

Text

Part I

妈妈： 玛丽， 你 喜欢 海鲜 吗？
Māma： Mǎlì, nǐ xǐhuan hǎixiān ma?

玛丽： 我喜欢海鲜， 也喜欢 青菜。
Mǎlì： Wǒ xǐhuan hǎixiān, yě xǐhuan qīngcài.

妈妈： 京京， 你呢？ 你吃什么？
Māma： Jīngjīng, nǐ ne? Nǐ chī shénme?

京京： 我喜欢 牛肉， 本 也 喜欢 牛肉。
Jīngjīng： Wǒ xǐhuan niúròu, Běn yě xǐhuan niúròu.

妈妈： 本， 你喜欢吃 鱼 吗？
Māma： Běn, nǐ xǐhuan chī yú ma?

本： 我喜欢吃鱼。
Běn： Wǒ xǐhuan chī yú.

妈妈： 京京， 你吃米饭吗？
Māma： Jīngjīng, nǐ chī mǐfàn ma?

京京： 我不要 米饭， 我要 面条。
Jīngjīng： Wǒ bú yào mǐfàn, wǒ yào miàntiáo.

本： 我也要面条， 我喜欢吃中国面条。
Běn： Wǒ yě yào miàntiáo, wǒ xǐhuan chī Zhōngguó miàntiáo.

妈妈： 这是面条。
Māma： Zhè shì miàntiáo.

京京和本： 谢谢！
Jīngjīng hé Běn： xièxie!

Mum: Mary, do you like seafood?

Mary: Yes, I like seafood and green vegetables, too.

Mum: Jingjing, how about you? What do you want to eat?

Jingjing: I like beef, so does Ben.

Mum: Ben, do you like to eat fish?

Ben: Yes, I like to eat fish.

Mum: Jingjing, do you want rice?

Jingjing: No, I don't want rice. I want noodles.

Ben: I also want noodles. I like Chinese noodles.

Mum: Here are the noodles.

Jingjing and Ben: Thank you.

Learning Tip

The modal verb 喜欢 can be followed by another verb to form a serial verb phrase. **For example,**
喜欢吃……
Like to eat ……

Grammar Point

1. 喜欢 is a verb that means 'like' or 'enjoy'. It can be followed by a noun. Use the following pattern:
   喜欢 + noun (someone/something)
   e.g. 我喜欢绿色。
   爸爸喜欢面条。
   喜欢 is also a special type of verb called a modal verb. It can also be followed by another verb (action).
   Use the following pattern:
   喜欢 + verb (action)
   e.g. 我喜欢吃海鲜。妈妈喜欢喝茶。

2. The adverb 也 means 'also/too'. 也 is always placed before the verb. Please note that you CANNOT use 也 to connect words or sentences.
   e.g. 我喜欢牛肉，他也喜欢牛肉。(√)
   我喜欢牛肉，也，他喜欢牛肉。(×)

Part II

他喜欢吃中国面条

丽丽是我的朋友，她家在伦敦。大卫也是我的朋友，他家也在伦敦。丽丽喜欢海鲜，她也喜欢青菜。大卫喜欢吃牛肉，我也喜欢牛肉。我喜欢吃面条，大卫也喜欢吃面条，我们都喜欢吃中国面条。

Exercises

Listen 1 Number the following items in the order that they are played in the recording.

Listen 2 Listen to the recording and put a cross (X) in the correct boxes.

	seafood	vegetable	beef	noodles	rice	fish
Mary	X					
David						
I						
mother						
father						

Read 3 Read the sentences and match them with the correct pictures.

| | 玛丽喜欢海鲜。 | | 大卫喜欢牛肉。 | | 京京也喜欢吃鱼。 |

| | 大卫要面条。 | | 妈妈喜欢吃米饭。 | | 玛丽也喜欢青菜。 |

Read 4 Read the text and complete the gap in each sentence using a word from the box below. There are more words than gaps.

这是我的小狗，他叫小黄。小黄喜欢喝牛奶，也喜欢吃牛肉。那是我的小猫，她叫咪咪。咪咪也喜欢喝牛奶，她不吃肉，她喜欢吃鱼。我喜欢我的小狗和小猫。

咪咪 Mī mī | Seafood | soft drink | rice | juice | beef | noodles | milk | Xiaohuang | fish | eggs

vegetable | fruit | tea | Xiao gou | Xiao mao

1) My dog is called ....

2) Xiaohuang likes to eat ....

3) Xiaohuang likes to drink ....

4) My cat likes to eat .... , doesn't like to eat ....

Speak
5

Talk about the pictures in Chinese.

	鱼	海鲜	牛肉	青菜	面条	米饭
京京吃什么？		✕				
姐姐吃什么？						
哥哥吃什么？						
妈妈吃什么？						
爸爸吃什么？						
每个人都吃什么？						

e.g. 京京吃什么？京京吃海鲜。

Speak
6

Role play. Ask your partner what his/her family members like to eat.

| 海鲜 | 牛肉 | 鱼 | 鸡蛋 | 米饭 | 面条 | 青菜 |

e.g. 你妈妈喜欢吃什么？我妈妈喜欢吃鱼。

你爸爸喜欢吃什么？我爸爸喜欢吃中国面条。

Write 7 Complete the sentences with appropriate Chinese characters.

1）我吃海鲜，□□吃青菜。

2）我喜欢吃□□条。

3）我吃□□饭，你呢？

4）妈妈吃绿色的蔬□。

5）我喜欢吃鱼，姐姐也喜欢吃□。

6）他喜欢吃牛□。

7）爸爸喜欢吃□□面条。(Chinese noodles)

8）他喜欢海鲜，我□喜欢海鲜。

Write 8 Translate the following sentences into English.

1）你喜欢海鲜吗？..

2）姐姐喜欢吃鱼。..

3）哥哥喜欢牛肉。..

4）每个人都喜欢面条。..

5）面条很好，谢谢！..

Write 9 Translate the following sentences into Chinese.

1）This is my elder brother.

....

2）Lily is my friend. David is my friend, too.

....

3）He likes Chinese noodles.

....

4）This fruit is big. Thank you!

....

Write 10 Practise Chinese characters.

 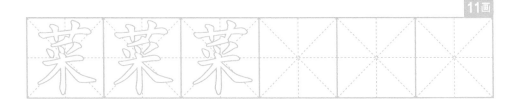

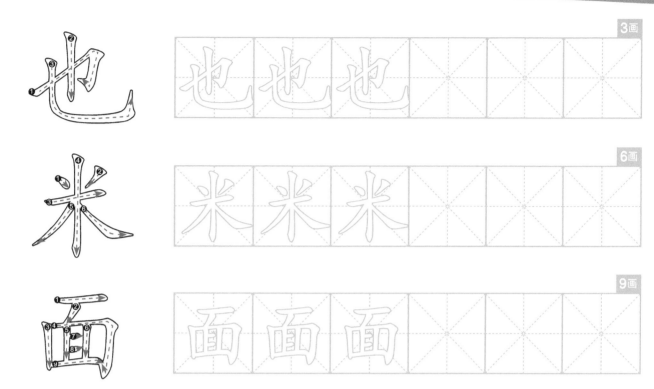

3画

也 也 也

6画

米 米 米

9画

面 面 面

文化常识 Cultural Tip

Chinese Cuisine

Chinese cuisine enjoys worldwide popularity because of its long history, rich variety and the numerous styles of cooking. Every region has its own distinctive flavours and ways of cooking.

Cuisine is so important to Chinese culture that it is referred to as 'Chinese food culture'.

Chinese cooking is focused on the 'five distinguishing elements of Chinese cuisine': colour, smell, taste, shape and meaning.

Every festival has its own special food. On birthdays, people eat longevity noodles that symbolise hope for a long life. In fact, the longer the noodle, the better luck the birthday boy or girl will have in the future.

第三单元小结　Unit Three Summary

Greetings

早上好。	Good morning.

Talking about food and drinks

你吃什么？ What would you like to eat? 你喝什么？ What would you like to drink?	Someone ＋ 吃 ＋ 什么？ Someone ＋ 喝 ＋ 什么？
他喝茶。He drinks tea. 我不喝咖啡。I don't drink coffee. 我吃面条。I eat noodles. 我不吃牛肉。I don't eat beef.	Someone ＋（不）喝 ＋ drinks Someone ＋（不）吃 ＋ food
每个人都喝茶。Everyone drinks tea. 每个人都吃早饭。Everyone eats breakfast.	每 ＋ measure word ＋ noun (something/ someone) ＋ 都 ＋ verb (action) ＋ noun

Talking about what you want

哥哥要海鲜。Elder brother wants seafood. 我不要蔬菜。I don't want vegetables.	Someone ＋ 要＋ noun（something） Someone ＋ 不要＋ noun（something）
你要水果吗？ Do you want fruit? 妈妈要咖啡吗？ Does mum want coffee?	Someone ＋ 要＋ noun ＋ 吗？

Asking reciprocal questions

我很好，你呢？ I am fine, how about you? 姐姐要海鲜，哥哥呢？ My elder sister wants seafood, how about my elder brother?	Topic (someone/something) ＋ 呢？

Adding description to something (noun)

绿色的蔬菜 green vegetables 红色的苹果 red apples	Adjective (description) ＋ 的 ＋ noun (something/someone)

Time phrase in a sentence

今天你吃什么？ 你今天吃什么？ What will you eat today?	time phrase ＋ someone ＋ verb … or someone ＋ time phrase ＋ verb …

Talking about likes

我喜欢牛肉。I like beef. 我喜欢吃牛肉。I like to eat beef.	Someone ＋ 喜欢 ＋ noun (someone/ something) Someone ＋ 喜欢 ＋ verb ＋ noun (someone/something)

第三单元小结　Unit Three Summary	
你喜欢海鲜吗? Do you like seafood? 你喜欢吃海鲜吗? Do you like to eat seafood?	Someone + 喜欢 + noun +吗? Someone + 喜欢 + verb + noun + 吗?
我喝咖啡，也喝茶。 I drink coffee and I also drink tea. 我喜欢海鲜，也喜欢菜。 I like seafood and I also like vegetables.	Someone + verb + noun, 也 + verb + noun
我喜欢牛肉，他也喜欢牛肉。 I like beef, he also likes beef. 爷爷喜欢米饭，奶奶也喜欢米饭。 Grandpa likes rice, grandma also likes rice.	Someone 1 + verb + noun, someone 2 也 + verb + noun

第十课 Lesson **10**

我们班有二十五个学生
There Are 25 Students in Our Class

Learning Objectives

交际话题 Topic of conversation:

班级和同学 Class and Classmates
Bānjí hé tóngxué

基本句型 Sentence patterns:

你们班有多少人？ 我们班有二十五个学生。
他们班有十一个男（学）生和九个女（学）生。

New Words

1 你们 nǐmen **pron.** you (plural)
2 我们 wǒmen **pron.** we, us
3 他们 tāmen **pron.** they, them
4 班 bān **n.** class
5 多少 duōshao **pron.** how many/much
6 百 bǎi **num.** hundred
7 学生 xuésheng **n.** student
8 男 nán **adj.** male
9 女 nǚ **adj.** female
10 男（学）生 nán(xué)sheng **n.** male student
11 女（学）生 nǚ(xué)sheng **n.** female student
12 二十 èrshí **num.** twenty
13 二十五 èrshíwǔ **num.** twenty-five

Numbers

Revision: 1-10

1	2	3	4	5	6	7	8	9	10
一	二	三	四	五	六	七	八	九	十
yī	èr	sān	sì	wǔ	liù	qī	bā	jiǔ	shí

Let's keep counting!

1-10		10 + 1...		2 x 10 + 1...		...	9 x 10 + 1...	
1	一	11	十一	21	二十一	...	91	九十一
2	二	12	十二	22	二十二	...	92	九十二
3	三	13	十三	23	二十三	...	93	九十三
4	四	14	十四	24	二十四	...	94	九十四
5	五	15	十五	25	二十五	...	95	九十五
6	六	16	十六	26	二十六	...	96	九十六
7	七	17	十七	27	二十七	...	97	九十七
8	八	18	十八	28	二十八	...	98	九十八
9	九	19	十九	29	二十九	...	99	九十九
10	十	20	二十	30	三十	...	100	一百 （yī bǎi）

Text

Part I

小雨： 京京，你们班有多少人？
Xiǎoyǔ： Jīngjīng， nǐmen bān yǒu duōshao rén？

京京： 我们班有二十个人。你们班呢？
Jīngjīng： Wǒmen bān yǒu èrshí gè rén. Nǐmen bān ne？

小雨： 我们班有二十五个学生。
Xiǎoyǔ： Wǒmen bān yǒu èrshíwǔ gè xuésheng.

> **Learning Tip**
>
> 1. 我们班有二十个人
> Have you noticed, in Chinese, instead of saying "There are 20 students in our class", we must say "Our class has 20 people".
>
> 2. "我们班" "你们班" "他们班"
> 'Our class, your (plural) class, their class' rather than 'my class, your (singular) class, his/her class'; this is because a class is always a group of students, not just one student.

京京： 有 多少 个 男学生？
Jīngjīng： Yǒu duōshao gè nán xuésheng?

小雨： 我们 班 有 十五 个 男学生。你们 呢？
Xiǎoyǔ： Wǒmen bān yǒu shíwǔ gè nán xuésheng. Nǐmén ne?

京京： 我们 班 有 十一 个 男学生。
Jīngjīng： Wǒmen bān yǒu shíyī gè nán xuésheng.

小雨： 有 多少 女学生？
Xiǎoyǔ： Yǒu duōshao nǚ xuésheng?

京京： 九 个 女学生。你们 班 有 多少 个 女学生？
Jīngjīng： Jiǔ gè nǚ xuésheng. Nǐmén bān yǒu duōshao gè nǚ xuésheng?

小雨： 我们 班 有 十 个 女学生。
Xiǎoyǔ： Wǒmen bān yǒu shí gè nǚ xuésheng.

京京： 我们 班 小，你们 班 大。
Jīngjīng： Wǒmen bān xiǎo, nǐmen bān dà.

Xiaoyu: Jingjing, how many students are there in your class?

Jingjing: There are 20 students in my class. How about your class?

Xiaoyu: There are 25 students in my class.

Jingjing: How many boys?

Xiaoyu: There are 15 boys in my class. How about yours?

Jingjing: There are 11 boys in my class.

Xiaoyu: How many girls?

Jingjing: Nine girls. How many girls are there in your class?

Xiaoyu: There are 10 girls in my class.

Jingjing: My class is small, yours is big.

Grammar Point

1. 多少 means 'how many' or 'how much'.
   It can be used to ask about any numbers or quantities.
   It can be used with or without a measure word when followed by a noun.
   e.g. 你们班有多少（个）人？
   In a question, 多少 is always in the same place in a sentence as where the answer will be.
   e.g 你们班有多少个女生？
   我们班有九个女生。

2. You will need to use 有 to say
   "There are......"
   我们班有二十个人。
   "Are there......?"
   你们班有二十人吗？
   "How many......are there?"
   你们班有多少人？

Part II

我们班有二十五个学生

我叫小雨，我和天天是同学。我家在北京，天天家在上海，我们都是中学生。我们班有二十五个学生，十五个男学生和十个女学生。他们班有二十个学生，十一个男生，九个女生。你们班呢？你们班有多少人？

Exercises

Listen 1 Listen to the recording and put a cross (X) in the correct boxes.

	25 students	20 students	9 female students	15 male students	11 male students	10 female students
our class	X					
their class						

Listen 2 Listen to the recording and use the words in the box to complete the sentences. There are more words than gaps.

female students	my class	students
male students	her class	your class

1) There are 12 male students in ....

2) There are 30 students in ....

3) How many .... are there in your class?

4) There aren't .... in my class.

TIPS

You might find it helpful to quickly read through the available answers and the sentences before the recording is played.

Speak **3** Role play. In pairs, ask each other how many male and female students are there in your class?

e.g. 我们班有多少个男生？　我们班有十个男生。

我们班有多少个女生？　我们班有十一个女生。

Speak **4** Talk about the picture in Chinese.

Describe the class in this picture. Such as, how many students are there in this class? How many male and female students are there in this class?

e.g. 我们这个班有…

Read
5

Read the sentences and match them with picture A or B.

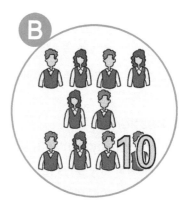

A:你们班有多少人?
B:我们班有二十个学生。

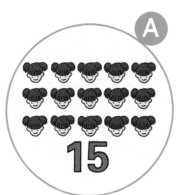

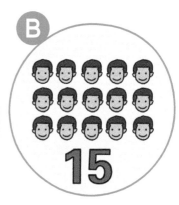

A:你们班有多少男学生?
B:我们班有十五个男学生。

A:你们班有多少女学生?
B:我们班有十二个女学生。

A:他们班有多少中国学生?
B:他们班有十四个中国学生。

Read 6　Read the following paragraph and answer the questions below in English.

　　我是中学生，我们班有二十六个学生，十五个男学生，十一个女学生。大海是我的朋友，他也是中学生。他们班有十三个人，六个男学生，七个女学生。我们班很大，他们班很小。

Questions:

1）How many students are there in our class?

2）How many boys are there in our class?

3）How many girls are there in our class?

4）Who is Dahai? How many students are there in Dahai's class?

5）How many students are there in Dahai's class?

Write 7　Complete the sentences with appropriate Chinese characters.

1）你 ☐ 班有多少人？　　　2）我们 ☐ 有十二个人。

3）他们班有 ☐ 少男学生？

4）大海他们班有三个 ☐ 学生，四个女学生。

5）京京有十一个 ☐ 同学，十个男同学。

Write 8　Translate the following sentences into English.

1）你们班有多少人？ ....

2）我们班有二十个学生。 ....

3）小雨有十二个女同学。 ....

4）大海有四个男同学。 ....

Write 9 Translate the following sentences into Chinese.

1） There are twenty students in my class. ....

2） How many friends do you have? ....

3） His has two dogs in his house. ....

4） My class is big, yours is small. ....

Write 10 Practise Chinese characters.

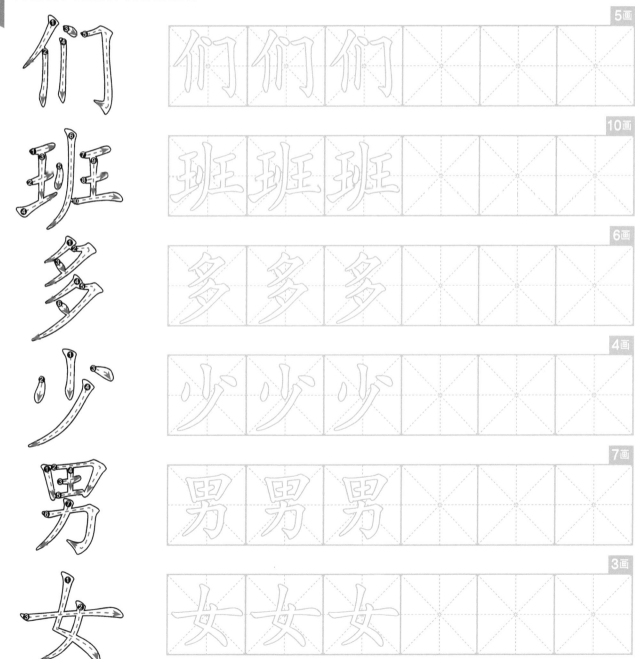

第十一课 Lesson **11**

星期三我有中文课
I Have a Chinese Class on Wednesday

Learning Objectives

交际话题 Topic of conversation:

课程表 Class Schedule
Kèchéngbiǎo

基本句型 Sentence patterns:

星期三我有中文课。　星期三我没有法文课。
现在几点(钟)?　现在八点一刻。

	1	2	3	4	5	6	7	8	9	10
Mon	Chinese 汉语	English 英语	Maths 数学	History 历史	Chemistry 化学	Chemistry 化学	Physics 物理	Physics 物理		Maths 数学
Tue	Music 音乐	Music 音乐	Religion Study 宗教	Physics 物理	P.E. 体育	P.E. 体育			Biology 生物	Biology 生物
Wed	Maths 数学	History 历史	Music 音乐	Music 音乐		Physics 物理	English 英语	History 历史	Chemistry 化学	
Thu	Maths 数学	Chinese 汉语	Latin 拉丁语	Latin 拉丁语	Physics 物理	Physics 物理				
Fri	Chinese 汉语	Religion Study 宗教	English 英语	Maths 数学	Latin 拉丁语					

New Words

1 星期三 xīngqīsān　n. Wednesday

2 星期四 xīngqīsì　n. Thursday

3 中文 Zhōngwén　n. Chinese

4 法文 Fǎwén　n. French

5 课 kè　n. class

6 现在 xiànzài　n. now

7 点 diǎn　mw. o'clock

8 半 bàn　num. half

9 分 fēn　m.w. minute

10 刻 kè　m.w. quarter

11 明天 míngtiān　n. tomorrow

12 零 líng　num. zero

Days of the Week

What day is it today?

今天星期几？
jīntiān xīngqī jǐ

今天星期…
jīntiān xīngqī

星期 + number 1 – 6

Sunday

MONDAY	星 期 一 xīngqī yī
TUESDAY	星 期 二 xīngqī èr
WEDNESDAY	星 期 三 xīngqī sān

THURSDAY	星 期 四 xīngqī sì
FRIDAY	星 期 五 xīngqī wǔ
SATURDAY	星 期 六 xīngqī liù

| SUNDAY | 星 期 日 xīngqī rì |
| | 星 期 天 xīngqī tiān |

Time

What's the time?

现在几点？
xiànzài jǐ diǎn ?

现在…
xiànzài

现在一点
yī diǎn

现在两点
liǎng diǎn

现在三点一刻
sān diǎn yī kè

现在四点半
sì diǎn bàn

现在十一点零五分
shí yī diǎn líng wǔ fèn

现在十二点四十五分
shí èr diǎn sì shí wǔ

Text

Part I

京京：妈妈，早上好！
Jīngjīng： Māma, zǎoshang hǎo!

妈妈：早上好！你吃什么？
Māma： Zǎoshang hǎo! Nǐ chī shénme?

京京：我吃面包和鸡蛋。
Jīngjīng： Wǒ chī miànbāo hé jīdàn.

妈妈：要苹果和蔬菜吗？
Māma： Yào píngguǒ hé shūcài ma?

京京：我要这个红苹果。
Jīngjīng： Wǒ yào zhège hóng píngguǒ.

妈妈：喝什么？
Māma： Hē shénme?

京京：我喜欢喝果汁，那个粉红色的果汁。
Jīngjīng： Wǒ xǐhuan hē guǒzhī, nàge fěnhóngsè de guǒzhī.

妈妈：我也喜欢那个果汁。
Māma： Wǒ yě xǐhuan nàge guǒzhī.

京京：妈妈，现在几点（钟）？
Jīngjīng： Māma, xiànzài jǐ diǎn (zhōng)?

妈妈：现在八点一刻。
Māma： Xiànzài bā diǎn yí kè.

京京：今天星期几？
Jīngjīng： Jīntiān xīngqī jǐ?

妈妈：今天星期三。你有什么课？
Māma： Jīntiān xīngqīsān. Nǐ yǒu shénme kè?

京京：星期三我有中文课。
Jīngjīng： Xīngqīsān wǒ yǒu Zhōngwén kè.

妈妈：今天你有法文课吗？
Māma： Jīntiān nǐ yǒu Fǎwén kè ma?

京京：星期三我没有法文课，
Jīngjīng： Xīngqīsān wǒ méiyǒu Fǎwén kè,

　　　星期四我有法文课。
　　　xīngqīsì wǒ yǒu Fǎwén kè.

Jingjing: Good morning, mum!
Mum: Good morning. What will you eat?
Jingjing: I will eat bread and egg.
Mum: Do you want an apple and vegetables?
Jingjing: I want this red apple.
Mum: What do you drink?
Jingjing: I like to drink juice, the pink juice.
Mum: I like that juice, too.
Jingjing: Mum, what time is it now?
Mum: It is 8:15.
Jingjing: What day is today?
Mum: Today is Wednesday. What class do you have today?
Jingjing: I have a Chinese class on Wednesday.
Mum: Do you have a French class today?
Jingjing: I don't have French class on Wednesday. I have a French class on Thursday.

Brain Teaser

1. How is 几 different from 多少？

2. Can you spot the difference in the sentence order between Chinese and English?
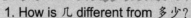
星期三我有中文课。
I have a Chinese class on Wednesday.

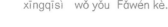

Grammar Point

1. Two o'clock is 两点 instead of 二点。

2. You only need to add 零 (0) in front of the number if the minute number is less than 10.
   e.g. 5:05 五点零五分; 8:10 八点十分

3. 几 means 'how many'. It is only used to ask about numbers less than 10. This character must be placed before a measure word and a noun.
   e.g. 你家有几个房间?

几 is always in the same place in the question as where the answer will go.
e.g. 今天星期几? 今天星期三
　　　现在几点? 现在四点。

Part II

今天我有中文课

　　我叫大卫，我是中学生，我家在伦敦。今天是星期三，早上九点零五分有中文课，我喜欢中文。今天我没有法文课。明天星期四，十点半我有法文课。我也喜欢法文。我们班有二十三个同学，他们都喜欢中文课。

Exercises

Listen 1 Listen to the recording and put a cross (X) in the correct boxes.

	in Beijing	Chinese class	8:30 am	France	French class
Chinese teacher's home					
French teacher is from					
Monday					
Wednesday					
It is					

Listen
2

Listen to the recording and choose the correct answer for each question.

1) What time is it?

☐	7:30
☐	7:00
☐	7:15
☐	7:05

2) What day is it today?

☐	Wednesday
☐	Sunday
☐	Thursday
☐	Friday

Speak
3

Role play. Ask your partner what day it is and what classes he/she has today.

> **e.g.** 今天星期几？　今天星期三。
>
> 你有什么课？　我有中文课。

Speak
4

Talk about the pictures in Chinese.

e.g. 星期三天天有法文课。

	天天	小雨	丽丽	大卫	本和同学
星期一					
星期二					
星期三	×				
星期四					
星期五					

小雨　　　　大卫　　　　天天

丽丽　　　　本和他的同学

Read **5** Read the sentences and match them with the correct pictures.

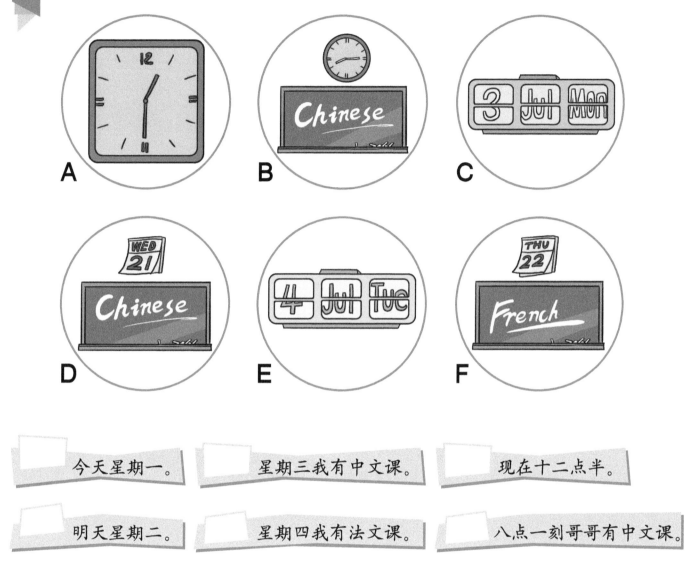

今天星期一。	星期三我有中文课。	现在十二点半。	
明天星期二。	星期四我有法文课。	八点一刻哥哥有中文课。	

Read **6** Read the following paragraph and fill in the blanks in English.

　　我叫京京，他叫大海，我们都是中学生。今天星期一，十点半我们都有课。我有中文课，大海没有中文课，他有法文课。我的中文老师是中国人，大海的法文老师是法国人。

1) Today is .... (which day of the week).

2) I have .... class.

3) Dahai has .... class.

4) We both have classes at ....

5) My Chinese teacher comes from ....

6) Dahai's French teacher comes from ....

Write 7 Complete the sentences with appropriate Chinese characters.

1）现在 ⬜ 点(钟)?

2）现在八点零五 ⬜ 。

3）你有中 ⬜ 课吗?

4）今天 ⬜ 期二， 八点 ⬜ 我有中文课。

5）法文老师一 ⬜ 半有课。

Write 8 Translate the following sentences into English.

1）现在几点(钟)? ....

2）现在十点半。 ....

3）明天八点一刻我有课。 ....

4）星期三我有中文课。 ....

5）星期四我没有法文课。 ....

Write 9 Translate the following sentences into Chinese.

1） I have a Chinese class on Monday.

....

2） I eat bread and drink milk in the morning.

....

3）It's 10 o'clock now.

....

4）Is your teacher Chinese?

....

Write
10

Practise Chinese characters.

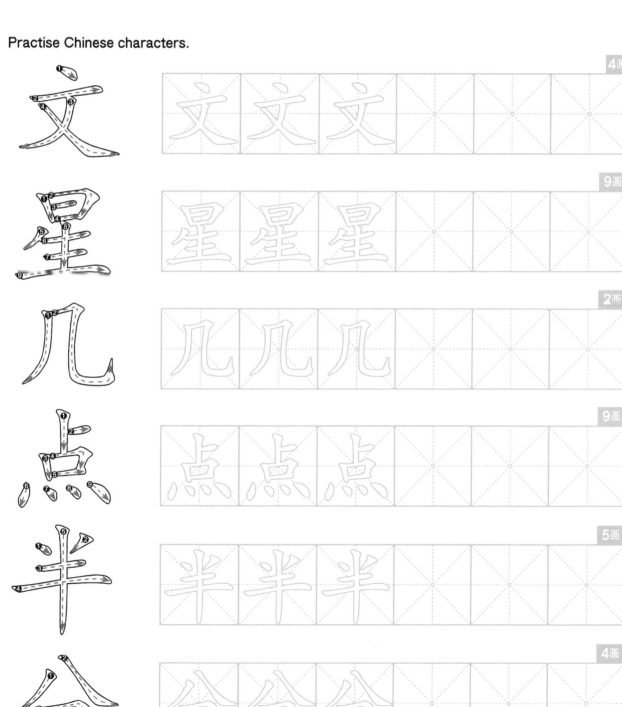

第十二课 (Lesson) **12**

A Day at School　学校的一天

Learning Objectives

交际话题 Topic of conversation:

学校的一天　A Day at School
Xuéxiào de yì tiān

基本句型 Sentence patterns:

你几点上课？　我八点一刻上课。
这是我要的书。你喜欢读书吗？

New Words

1	上课 shàng kè	go to class	7 中 zhōng	n. middle
2	下课 xià kè	finish class	8 下 xià	n. down, below
3	上午 shàngwǔ	n. morning	9 读 dú	v. to read
4	中午 zhōngwǔ	n. noon	10 本 běn	m.w. (a measure word for books)
5	下午 xiàwǔ	n. afternoon	11 书 shū	n. book
6	上 shàng	n. up, top	12 休息 xiūxi	v. to rest

Text

Part I

(上学路上)
shàngxué lù shang

姐姐： 小雨，你几点上课？
Jiějie: Xiǎoyǔ, nǐ jǐ diǎn shàng kè?

小雨： 我八点一刻上课。
Xiǎoyǔ: Wǒ bā diǎn yí kè shàng kè.

姐姐： 今天上午你有什么课？
Jiějie: Jīntiān shàngwǔ nǐ yǒu shénme kè?

小雨： 我有中文课。
Xiǎoyǔ: Wǒ yǒu Zhōngwén kè.

姐姐： 你有法文课吗？
Jiějie: Nǐ yǒu Fǎwén kè ma?

小雨： 我今天没有法文课，
Xiǎoyǔ: Wǒ jīntiān méiyǒu Fǎwén kè,

　　　　星期二有法文课。
　　　　xīngqī'èr yǒu Fǎwén kè.

姐姐： 你今天几点下课？
Jiějie: Nǐ jīntiān jǐ diǎn xià kè?

小雨： 我中午十二点半下课。
Xiǎoyǔ: Wǒ zhōngwǔ shí'èr diǎn bàn xià kè.

姐姐： 下午上课吗？
Jiějie: Xiàwǔ shàng kè ma?

小雨： 下午没有课，下午休息。
Xiǎoyǔ: Xiàwǔ méiyǒu kè, xiàwǔ xiūxi.

Learning Tip

You might have noticed 上 and 下 appeared a few times in this lesson. 上 on its own means 'up, top'; 下 on its own means 'down, below'. When followed by a noun, these characters can have rather different meanings.

Brain Teaser

我中午十二点半下课。
I finish class at 12:30, at noon.
Can you spot the difference in the sentence order between Chinese and English?

(On the way to school)

Elder sister: Xiaoyu, What time do you go to class?

Xiaoyu: I go to class at 8:15.

Elder sister: What classes do you have this morning?

Xiaoyu: I have a Chinese class.

Elder sister: Do you have a French class?

Xiaoyu: No, I don't have a French class.
　　　　French class is on Tuesday.

Elder sister: What time do you finish your class today?

Xiaoyu: At 12:30, at noon.

Elder sister: Do you have class this afternoon?

Xiaoyu: I don't have class this afternoon. It is break time.

（在图书馆）
Zài túshūguǎn

小雨：　你好！这是我要的书。
Xiǎoyǔ：　Nǐ hǎo! Zhè shì wǒ yào de shū.

管理员：　几本书？
Guǎnlǐyuán：　Jǐ běn shū?

小雨：　三本。
Xiǎoyǔ：　Sān běn.

管理员：　你喜欢读书吗？
Guǎnlǐyuán：　Nǐ xǐhuan dú shū ma?

小雨：　我喜欢读书。
Xiǎoyǔ：　Wǒ xǐhuan dú shū.

(In the library)
Xiaoyu: Hello! These are the books that I want.
Librarian: How many are there?
Xiaoyu: Three, please.
Librarian: Do you like reading?
Xiaoyu: Yes, I like reading.

Brain Teaser:

本 is the measure word for books.
What are the other measure words you have learned so far and what are they used for?

Grammar Point

我要的书。
The books that I want.
When you want to describe something, you need to use 的. The order should be:
Description + 的 + the thing you want to describe
e.g. 我要 (I want) + 的 + 书 (book)。

Part II

我喜欢读书

　　我是天天，我家在中国上海，我喜欢读书。今天是星期五，我上午八点上课，中午十二点半下课。今天我有中文课和法文课。我喜欢上课，也喜欢读书。我有四本中文书，一本法文书。下午我没有课，我休息，在家读书。

Exercises

Listen 1 Listen to the recording and put a cross (X) in the correct boxes.

	8:00 am	9:30 am	10:00 am	11:00 am	12:30 pm	2:45 pm	5:00 pm
Xiaoyu							
elder sister							
Dahai							
elder brother							
the teacher							

Listen 2 Choose from the following morning, noon, and afternoon to complete the sentences. Some words can be used several times.

1）I have Chinese lesson this . . . .

3）There is no class this . . . .

2）I do not have French lesson this . . . .

4）I finish class at 12:30, at . . . .

Speak 3 Role play. Find out what time your partner will have breakfast (吃早饭) today.
chīzǎofàn

e.g. 今天你几点吃早饭？今天我下午六点吃早饭。

Speak 4 Talk about the following timetable by asking and answering questions.

e.g. 你星期一上午有什么课？ 我星期一上午有中文课。
星期二你几点上法文课？星期二我上午十点上法文课。

	星期一	星期二	星期三	星期四	星期五	星期六	星期日
上午 7:00-7:30				吃早饭			
上午 8:00-8:45	中文课		法文课		中文课		读书
上午 10:00-10:45		法文课		中文课			
中午 12:00				下课			
下午 12:30-2:00				吃饭			休息
下午 2:30-5:45				读书			

Read 5 Read the sentences and match them with the correct pictures.

A

B

C

D

E

F

	我八点上课。
	姐姐十二点半下课。
	老师下午五点休息。

	小雨喜欢读书。
	这是我要的中文书。
	我有三本法语书。

Read 6 Read the following paragraph and choose the correct answer(s) to the questions below in English.

　　这是小雨的房间。小雨的房间有中文书，也有法文书。小雨很喜欢读书。今天是星期天，小雨没有课，她上午在家读书，下午喝咖啡、休息。

1）What are there in Xiaoyu's room?

　　A. Chinese books　　B. French books　　C. Bread　　D. A cat

2）What does Xiaoyu like?

　　A. Drinking coffee　　B. Rest　　C. Going to classes　　D. Reading books

3）What day is today?

　　A. Monday　　B. Wednesday　　C. Sunday　　D. Saturday

4）Does Xiaoyu have class today?

　　A. Yes　　B. No

5）What does Xiaoyu do on Sunday?

　　A. Go to class　　B. Drink coffee　　C. Read　　D. Rest

Write **7** Complete the sentences with appropriate Chinese characters.

1）我上午有课，[ ]午没有课。

4）我有十五本 [ ]，你呢?

2）你今天上 [ ] 几点上课?

5）你喜 [ ] 读书吗?

3）你有几 [ ] 书?

6）我 [ ] 欢读书。

Write **8** Translate the following sentences into English.

1）你几点上课? ....

2）我八点上课。 ....

3）你喜欢这本书吗? ....

4）我有三本中文书。 ....

Write **9** Translate the following sentences into Chinese.

1） I like reading.

....

2） I don't have a French class on Tuesday.

....

3） The breakfast is at 7 o'clock in the morning.

....

4） Today is Sunday. It's break time.

....

Write
10

Practise Chinese characters.

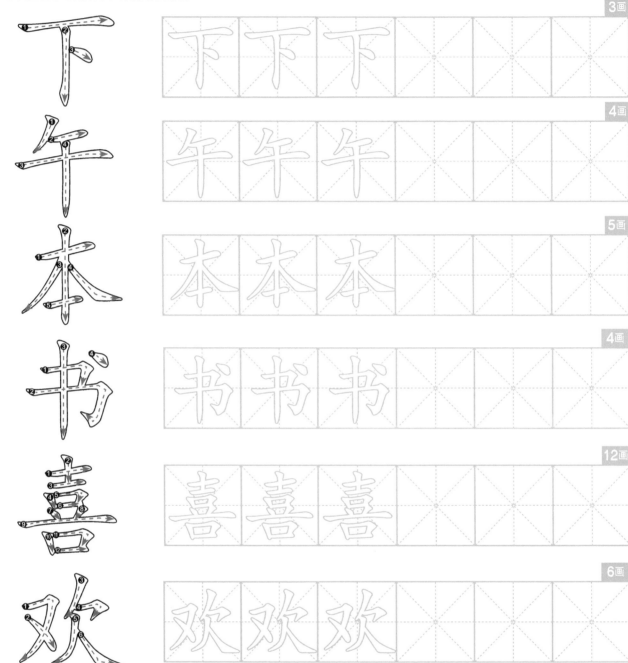

文化常识 Cultural Tip

The Chinese schooling system

In China, there are six years of primary school, three years of middle school (Year 7 to Year 9), and three years of high school (Year 10 to Year 12). There is an exam at the end of middle school to decide who can attend the best high schools. This exam is called 中考 zhōng kǎo. It is a very competitive exam and students often work extremely hard to prepare for it.

第四单元小结　Unit Four　Summary

Numbers 10 +	
十一，十二，…. 十九	11 – 19：10+1，2，…9
二十，二十一…. 九十九	20 – 99：2x10，2X10+1，… 9x10+9

Days of the week	
星期一，星期二…星期六	Monday, Tuesday... Saturday
星期天 or 星期日	Sunday
今天星期几？What day is it today?	今天 + 星期 + 几?
今天星期三。Today is Wednesday.	今天 + 星期 + number

Talking about your class	
我们班　　你们班　　他们班	my class　　your class　　his/her class
你们班有多少人？ How many students are there in your class? 伦敦有多少人？ How many people are there in London?	Somewhere + 有 + 多少 + 人?
我们班有二十五个学生。 There are 25 students in my class. 我们班有十个男学生和十五个女学生。 There are 10 boys and 15 girls in my class.	Somewhere + 有 + number + 人
几：how many 你家有几个房间？ How many rooms are there in your house?	几 + measure word + noun (someone/something) Often used with number less than 10
多少：how many 你们班有多少（个）学生？ How many students are there in your class?	多少 (+ measure word)+ noun. Often used with any numbers

Talking about class schedules	
星期三我有中文课。 I have a Chinese class on Wednesday. 星期五妹妹有英文课。 My younger sister has an English class on Friday.	Time phrase + someone + 有 + subject + 课

星期三我没有法文课。 I don't have French class on Wednesday. 星期一哥哥没有中文课。 My elder brother doesn't have Chinese class on Monday.	Time phrase + someone + 没有 + subject + 课
Talking about time	
现在几点? What time is it?	现在 + 几 + 点?
现在七点。It's 7 o'clock.	现在 + number + 点。
现在八点半。 It's half past 8.	现在 + number + 点 + 半。
现在九点一刻。 It is a quarter past 9.	现在 + number + 点 + 一刻。
现在十一点四十五分。 It is 11:45.	现在 + number + 点 + number of number of minutes + 分
你几点上课? What time do you go to class? 姐姐几点上课? What time does my elder sister go to class?	someone + 几点 + 上课?
我八点上课。 I go to class at 8 o'clock. 小雨九点半上课。 Xiaoyu goes to class at 9:30.	someone + number + 点 + 上课 (somone + time + action)
Describing something	
我要的书。The book that I want. 你喜欢的猫。The cat that you like.	Description + 的 + the thing you want to describe
Measure words	
几本书? How many books?	几 + measure word + noun
三本。 Three.	Number + 本

第十三课 Lesson **13**

I Go to the Gymnasium 我去体育馆

Learning Objectives

交际话题 Topic of conversation:

课外活动 Extracurricular activities
Kèwài huódòng

基本句型 Sentence patterns:

你的生日是几月几号？ 我的生日是5月21号。
我去图书馆。 我去看书。

New Words

1 生日 shēngrì n. birthday

2 月 yuè n. month

3 号／日 hào/rì n. date

4 去 qù v. to go

5 体育馆 tǐyùguǎn n. gymnasium, stadium

6 图书馆 túshūguǎn n. library

7 看书 kàn shū v. to read books

8 跑步 pǎobù v. to run; jogging

9 教室 jiàoshì n. classroom

10 运动场 yùndòngchǎng n. sports ground, athletic ground

Months of the Year

Number 1-12 + 月
yuè

JANUARY	一	月
FEBRUARY	二	月
MARCH	三	月
... ...		
OCTOBER	十	月
NOVEMBER	十一	月
DECEMBER	十二	月

Dates of the Month

Number + 日／号
rì　hào

1ST	一	日	一	号
2ND	二	日	二	号
3RD	三	日	三	号
... ...				
29TH	二十九	日	二十九	号
30TH	三十	日	三十	号
31ST	三十一	日	三十一	号

Text

Part I

大海：　小雨，你的生日是几月几号？
Dàhǎi：　Xiǎoyǔ,　nǐ de shēngrì shì jǐ yuè jǐ hào？

小雨：　我的生日是 5 月 21 号。
Xiǎoyǔ：　Wǒ de shēngrì shì wǔ yuè èrshíyī hào.

大海：　5 月 21 号？今天是 5 月几号？
Dàhǎi：　Wǔ yuè èrshíyī hào？ Jīntiān shì wǔ yuè jǐ hào？

小雨：　今天是 5 月 16 号，星期五。
Xiǎoyǔ：　Jīntiān shì wǔ yuè shíliù hào,　xīngqīwǔ.

大海：　星期五下午没有课，我去体育馆，你去吗？
Dàhǎi：　Xīngqīwǔ xiàwǔ méiyǒu kè,　wǒ qù tǐyùguǎn,　nǐ qù ma？

小雨：　我不去体育馆，我去图书馆，我去看书。
Xiǎoyǔ：　Wǒ bú qù tǐyùguǎn,　wǒ qù túshūguǎn,　wǒ qù kàn shū.

大海：　我去跑步。
Dàhǎi：　Wǒ qù pǎobù.

Learning Tip

When translating, a 'word for word' approach rarely works. It is important to remember the meaning of new words, but it is also important to remember what a whole phrase means.
e.g. 你的生日是几月几号？
'Your birthday is which month which date?' = 'When is your birthday?'

Dahai: When is your birthday, Xiaoyu?

Xiaoyu: My birthday is on 21st of May.

Dahai: 21st of May. What date is it today?

Xiaoyu: It is Friday, 16th of May.

Dahai: We don't have class on Friday afternoon. I am going to the gym. Do you want to come with me?

Xiaoyu: No, I don't want to go to the gym. I'd like to go to the library and read some books.

Dahai: I will go jogging.

Grammar Point

1. In Chinese, think big first! Large units (like years) go before smaller units (like months or the date). Is this different to English? Have a look at the following pattern:
Month - date - days of the week.
e.g. 今天是5月16号，星期五。

2. We've already learnt 几 in lesson 4. 几 is always in the same position as the answer. Here is no different.
e.g. 你的生日是几月几号？
我的生日是3月5号。

Part II

她去看书，他去跑步

这是我们的教室，他们是我的同学。这是小雨，她是北京人，她的生日是5月21号。那是大海，他是香港人，他的生日是5月29号。小雨喜欢看书，她每天去图书馆，她去看书。大海喜欢跑步，他喜欢去运动场，他去跑步。

Exercises

Listen 1 Listen to the recording and put a cross (X) in the correct boxes.

	12 Nov	10 Aug	11 Dec	jogging	reading	gymnasium	sports ground	classroom	library
today									
mother's birthday									
father's birthday									
Xiaoyu									
Jingjing									
elder brother									
younger sister									

Listen 2 Listen to the recording and put a cross (X) in the correct box.

1) Today's date is ....

☐	31 March
☐	18 March
☐	31 August
☐	13 August

3) In the morning, I am going to ....

☐	read books
☐	go to the stadium
☐	have Chinese noodles
☐	go running

2) Today is ....

☐	Friday
☐	Thursday
☐	Wednesday
☐	Tuesday

4) In the afternoon, I am going to ....

☐	read books
☐	go to the stadium
☐	have Chinese noodles
☐	go running

Read 3 Read the sentences and match them with the correct pictures.

A

B

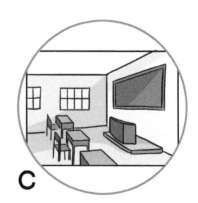

C

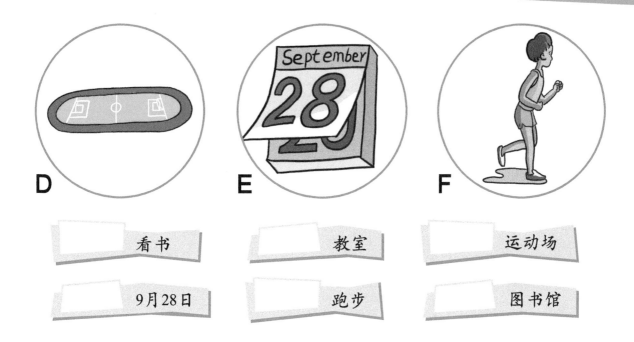

D | E | F

看书

教室

运动场

9月28日

跑步

图书馆

Read 4 Read the following paragraph and answer the questions below in English.

　　今天是7月25日，星期六。今天是我的生日，也是哥哥的生日。我喜欢看书，上午，我和朋友去图书馆，我们去看书。哥哥喜欢跑步，他和朋友去体育馆，他们去跑步。中午我们和爸爸妈妈吃面条。我喜欢我的生日。

Questions:

1) What date is it today?

2) Whose birthday is it today?

3) What do I like and what do I do this morning?

4) What does my elder brother like doing?

5) What does my elder brother do this morning?

6) What do we have for lunch?

Speak 5 Talk about the pictures below. Tell your partner what activities the students are going to do and where they will be doing them.

e.g. 他去图书馆看书。

Speak 6 Role play. Find out when your partner's birthday is.

e.g. 你的生日是几月几号？

我的生日是…月…号。

Write 7 Complete the sentences with appropriate Chinese characters.

1）□□ 是星期五。

2）12 □ 25 □ 我们没有课。

3）今天是妈妈的 □□ 。

4）我 □ 教室，你去哪儿？

5）他喜欢 □ 书，他 □ 图书馆。

6）今天是 □ 月 □ 号？　今天是八月十五号。

Write 8 Translate the following paragraph into English.

　　这是我哥哥，他叫Thomas。他是英国人。他家在伦敦。今天是九月一号星期五，也是我哥哥的生日！他今天上午八点半上课，十点去图书馆。中午12点他和朋友去跑步。下午五点我们和爸爸妈妈去吃中国面条。

....

....

....

Write 9 Translate the following sentences into Chinese.

1) She goes running.

....

2) His birthday is 8 December.

....

3) He is not going to the stadium, he is going to the library.

....

4) We are going to his house to have tea.

....

Write 10 Practise Chinese characters.

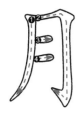

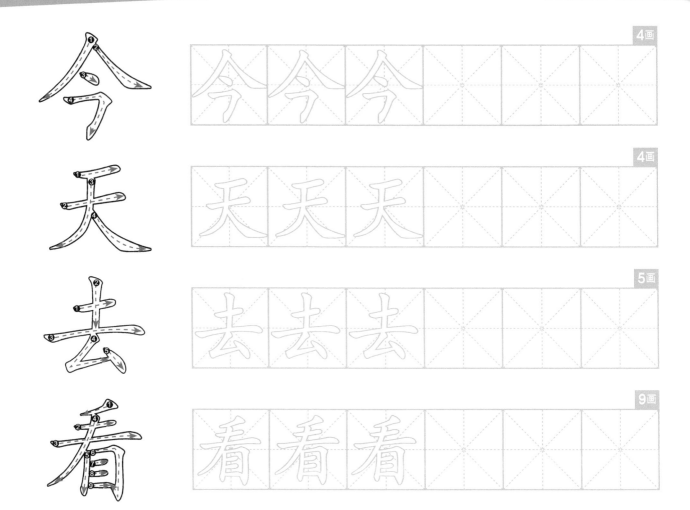

4画

4画

5画

9画

China's National Ball Game - Table Tennis

Table tennis was introduced into China in the early twentieth century. So many people loved the game that it became one of the most popular ball sports in China. There are now lots of famous Chinese table tennis players, and China has more than a few world champion players. It is no wonder table tennis is called the national ball game of China.

第十四课 Lesson

I Can Play Table Tennis 我会打乒乓球

14

Learning Objectives

交际话题 Topic of conversation:

体育活动 Sports Activities
Tǐyù huódòng

基本句型 Sentence patterns:

这是什么？　　　这是足球。　　哪个好？
我不会打乒乓球，会打网球。　　他跑得很快。

New Words

1 足球 zúqiú n. football, soccer

2 篮球 lánqiú n. basketball

3 打 dǎ v. to hit; to play (other ball games than football)

4 哪 nǎ pron. which

5 会 huì v. can; to be able to; to have the skill to

6 踢 tī v. to kick; to play (football)

7 网球 wǎngqiú n. tennis

8 乒乓球 pīngpāngqiú n. table tennis, ping-pong

9 跑 pǎo v. to run

10 得 de part. (a structural particle)

11 快 kuài adj. fast, quick

12 游泳 yóuyǒng v./n. to swim; swimming

13 游 yóu v. to swim

Text

Part I

小雨： 大卫，这是什么？
Xiǎoyǔ： Dàwèi, zhè shì shénme？

大卫： 这是足球。
Dàwèi： Zhè shì zúqiú.

小雨： 你有篮球吗？
Xiǎoyǔ： Nǐ yǒu lánqiú ma？

大卫： 有。我喜欢打篮球，
Dàwèi： Yǒu. Wǒ xǐhuan dǎ lánqiú,

　　　 你看，我有三个篮球。
　　　 nǐ kàn, wǒ yǒu sān gè lánqiú.

小雨： 哪个好？
Xiǎoyǔ： Nǎ gè hǎo？

大卫： 这个好。你会打篮球吗？
Dàwèi： Zhège hǎo. Nǐ huì dǎ lánqiú ma？

小雨： 我不会。我喜欢网球和乒乓球。
Xiǎoyǔ： Wǒ bú huì. Wǒ xǐhuan wǎngqiú hé pīngpāngqiú.

Xiaoyu : What's this ?
David: This is a football.
Xiaoyu: Do you have a basketball ?
David: Yes, I do. I like playing basketball.
　　　　Look, I have three basketballs.
Xiaoyu: Which one is the best?
David : This one. Can you play basketball?
Xiaoyu: No, I can't. I like playing tennis and
　　　　table tennis.
David: I don't know how to play table tennis.
　　　　I can play tennis.
Xiaoyu: Shall we go to the gym and play tennis?
David: Sure. What time is it now?
Xiaoyu: 2:30.
David: No class in the afternoon.
　　　　Let's go to the gym and play tennis.
Xiaoyu: Great.

Brain Teaser

Look at the sentences below. How is the word order and sentence structure of Chinese questions different from English?
e.g. 这是什么？ 这是足球。
　　 哪个好？ 那个好。

大卫： 我不会打乒乓球，会打网球。
Dàwèi： Wǒ bú huì dǎ pīngpāngqiú, huì dǎ wǎngqiú.

小雨： 我们去体育馆，我们去打网球，好吗？
Xiǎoyǔ： Wǒmen qù tǐyùguǎn, Wǒmen qù dǎ wǎngqiú, hǎo ma？

大卫： 好。现在几点钟？
Dàwèi： Hǎo. Xiànzài jǐ diǎnzhōng？

小雨： 现在两点半。
Xiǎoyǔ： Xiànzài liǎng diǎn bàn.

大卫： 下午没有课，我们去体育馆，去打网球。
Dàwèi： Xiàwǔ méiyǒu kè, wǒmen qù tǐyùguǎn, qù dǎ wǎngqiú.

小雨： 好。
Xiǎoyǔ： Hǎo.

Grammar Point

1. In Chinese, you don't generally 'play' sports. Instead, we use 踢 'to kick' or 打 'to hit', depending on whether you are playing a sport with your feet or with hands and a bat. Remember the following pattern:
   踢 + football   打 + other ball sports
   e.g. 踢足球；打篮球；打网球；打乒乓球

2. 会 means 'can, to be able to, to have the skill to'. It is a modal verb. Modal verbs like 会 can be followed by another verb (action). 会 is only used for a skill that can be learned.
   会 + verb (skill) + noun (something)
   e.g. 会打网球；会踢足球

3. 得 is a structural particle. In this unit it is used with a verb and an adjective to show well or unwell the action is carried out. Use the following pattern:
   e.g. 打得很好；跑得快

4. 哪 'which' is a question word. It is often followed by a measure word.
   哪 + measure word + noun. (When the context is clear, the noun can be dropped)
   e.g. 哪个篮球好？
        这个。

Part II

我们也去体育馆

天天喜欢跑步，他跑得很快。天天喜欢游泳，他游得很快。天天也会打篮球、网球和乒乓球，他都打得很好。我们都喜欢天天。今天是星期六，姐姐去图书馆看书，天天去体育馆，他去打篮球。我们也去体育馆，我们也去打篮球。

Exercises

Listen 1

Listen to the recording and put a cross (X) in the correct boxes.

	basketball	football	table tennis	tennis	run	can swim	can't swim
this							
three							
my friend							
his younger sister							
father							
elder brother							
he							

Listen 2 Listen to the recording and answer the following questions in English.

1) What is Lily's relationship to me?

......

2) Where does Lily live?

......

3) How many cats does Lily have?

......

4) What activities can Lily do?

......

Read 3 Read the sentence and match it with picture A or B.

这是乒乓球。

他会打篮球。

我喜欢踢足球。

他不会打网球。

姐姐会游泳，
她游得很快。

哪个好?

Read 4 | Read the following paragraph then use the words in the box to complete the translation. There are words that you will not need to use.

今天是星期五，现在是十二点半，我们休息。下午两点我们有乒乓球课，我们都去体育馆。我们班有二十五个学生，十五个男同学，十个女同学。我们每个人都会打乒乓球，我们都打得很好。我们都喜欢乒乓球课。

| Saturday | Friday | Sunday | 12:00 | 12:30 | 11:30 | tennis | basketball |

| ping-pong | well | stadium | 15 | 10 | 25 |

Today is .... The time now is .... We have a .... lesson at 2pm. We are all going to the .... There are .... students in our class and we can all play ping-pong ....

Speak
5
Talk about the pictures below. Tell your partner what sports the students like or dislike.

e.g. 他喜欢游泳，他游得很快。

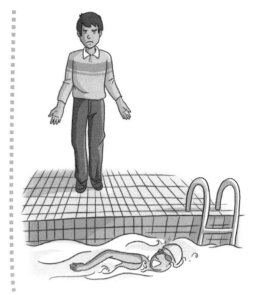

Speak
6
Role play. Tell your partner what activities and sports you can and can't do, and how well you can do them.

e.g. 我会踢足球。我踢得很好。

我不会打网球。我打得不好。

Write
7
Complete the sentences with appropriate Chinese characters.

1） 这是 ☐ ☐ ⚽ ，不是篮球。

2） 我喜欢 ☐ 网球，也喜欢 ☐ 乒乓 ☐ 。

3） 他 ☐ ☐ 游泳，他游得很 ☐ 。

4） 我的朋友喜欢跑步，他 ☐ 得很 ☐ 。

5） 我有三 ☐ 篮 ☐ ，十 ☐ 网 ☐ 。

6） 我喜欢 ☐ 足球，不喜欢打篮球。

7） ☐ 个苹果好? 这个好!

Write 8 Translate the following paragraph into English.

> 我家有四口人，我爸爸，我妈妈，我弟弟和我。爸爸喜欢看书。妈妈喜欢游泳。我和弟弟不会游泳，我们喜欢踢足球。我们都踢得很好。

....

....

Write 9 Translate the following sentences into Chinese.

1） I have two footballs and one basketball.

....

2） My elder sister and I are going to the stadium to play tennis.

....

3） Which apple is better?

....

4） My elder brother can swim. He swims fast.

....

Write
10

Practise Chinese characters.

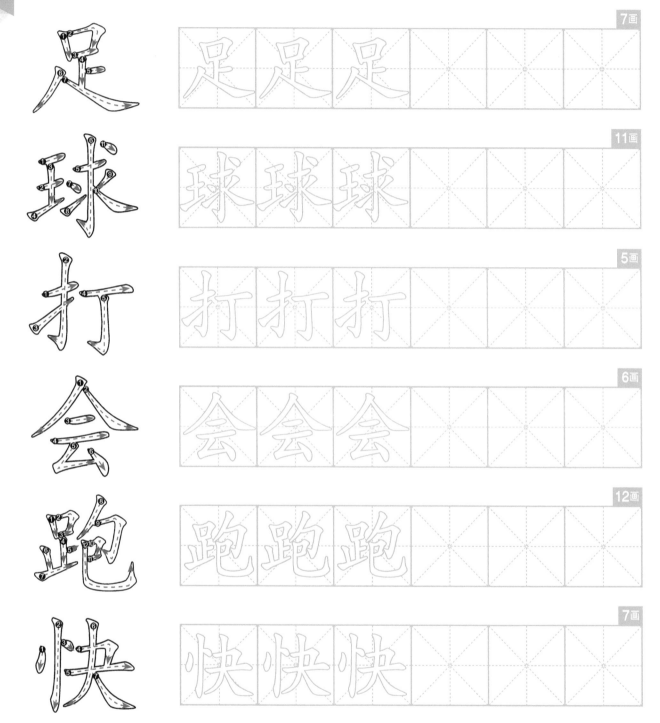

第十五课 Lesson

15

What's Your Hobby? 你的爱好是什么?

Learning Objectives

交际话题 Topic of conversation:

爱好 Hobbies
Àihào

基本句型 Sentence patterns:

你的爱好是什么？　你喜欢哪本书？
这本书。　　　　　他常常喝茶。

New Words

1. 爱好　àihào　n. hobby
2. 电子游戏　diànzǐ yóuxì　n. computer games
3. 玩　wán　v. to play (games)
4. 运动　yùndòng　n. sport, athletics
5. 听　tīng　v. to listen
6. 音乐　yīnyuè　n. music
7. 常常　chángcháng　adv. often
8. 上网　shàng wǎng　v. to surf the Internet
9. 看　kàn　v. to watch, to read
10. 电影　diànyǐng　n. film, movie

Text

Part I

大海： 小雨，你的爱好是什么？
Dàhǎi： Xiǎoyǔ， nǐ de àihào shì shénme？

小雨： 我的爱好是看书。
Xiǎoyǔ： Wǒ de àihào shì kàn shū.

大海： 你喜欢哪本书？
Dàhǎi： Nǐ xǐhuan nǎ běn shū？

小雨： 这本书。
Xiǎoyǔ： Zhè běn shū.

大海： 我也喜欢这本书。
Dàhǎi： Wǒ yě xǐhuan zhè běn shū.

小雨： 你的爱好是什么？
Xiǎoyǔ： Nǐ de àihào shì shénme？

大海： 我的爱好是玩电子游戏。
Dàhǎi： Wǒ de àihào shì wán diànzǐ yóuxì.

你玩电子游戏吗？
Nǐ wán diànzǐ yóuxì ma？

小雨： 我玩，星期日常常玩。
Xiǎoyǔ： Wǒ wán， xīngqīrì chángcháng wán.

大海： 你喜欢运动吗？
Dàhǎi： Nǐ xǐhuan yùndòng ma？

小雨： 我喜欢运动，我喜欢游泳，
Xiǎoyǔ： Wǒ xǐhuan yùndòng， wǒ xǐhuan yóuyǒng，

也喜欢打网球。
yě xǐhuan dǎ wǎngqiú.

大海： 我也喜欢运动，我喜欢打篮球，
Dàhǎi： Wǒ yě xǐhuan yùndòng， wǒ xǐhuan dǎ lánqiú，

也喜欢跑步。
yě xǐhuan pǎobù.

小雨： 星期六我们没有课，我们去体育馆。
Xiǎoyǔ： Xīngqīliù wǒmen méiyǒu kè， wǒmen qù tǐyùguǎn.

大海： 好，我们去打篮球，也打网球。
Dàhǎi： Hǎo， wǒmen qù dǎ lánqiú， yě dǎ wǎngqiú.

Learning Tip

In this lesson, we learn that 好 has another pronunciation. Similar to English, Chinese has words that have the same written form but are pronounced differently (and have different meanings). Sometimes it's important to use context and punctuation to figure out the correct meaning.

e.g. 你好；爱好
nǐ hǎo ài hào

Learning Tip

Add some flavour to your speaking and writing by using frequency words, such as 常常、每天. These words usually go before a verb, and they make sentences look smart!

Dahai: Xiaoyu, what's your hobby?
Xiaoyu: My hobby is reading.
Dahai: Which book do you like?
Xiaoyu: This book.
Dahai: I like this book, too.
Xiaoyu: What's your hobby?
Dahai: I like playing computer games. Do you like them?
Xiaoyu: Yes, I do. I often play on Sundays.
Dahai: Do you like sports?
Xiaoyu: I like sports. I like swimming and playing tennis.
Dahai: I also like sports. I like playing basketball and jogging.
Xiaoyu: We don't have class on Saturdays. Let's go to the gym.
Dahai: Great. Let's go play basketball and tennis.

Grammar Point

1. 常常 means 'often' or 'usually'. Words like this are called adverbs of frequency. They describe how often or regularly a verb (action) is carried out. Note, 常常 goes in front of the verb it describes. Use the following pattern:

常常 + verb

e.g. 哥哥的爱好是电影，他常常看电影。

爸爸不喜欢喝咖啡，他常常喝茶。

Part II

我们的爱好

我叫京京，我的爱好是运动。我常常跑步、游泳，我跑得很快，游得也很快。我妈妈喜欢听音乐，喜欢喝咖啡。爸爸不喝咖啡，他常常喝茶，他的爱好是上网。我哥哥不喜欢上网，也不喜欢运动，他的爱好是看电影，他常常看电影。

Exercises

Listen 1 Listen to the recording and put a cross (X) in the correct boxes.

	sport	hobby	listen to music	watch movies	surf the Internet	often read books	computer games
father							
we							
mother							
my younger sister							
Jingjing							
my friend							
he							

Listen 2 Listen to the recording and complete the gaps in each sentence using a word from the box below. There are more words than gaps.

playing tennis　surfing the internet　watching films　listening to music　reading books

do sports　playing basketball　juice　play computer games　playing football　swim

Chinese tea　English tea　coffee

1) I like to drink . . . .

2) My hobbies are . . . . and . . . .

3) I do not like . . . .

4) I can . . . . very well.

Read 3 Read the sentence and match it with picture A or B.

他的爱好是运动。

姐姐的爱好是听音乐。

哥哥玩电子游戏。

他喜欢哪本书？

我们去看电影。

他常常喝茶。

我不喜欢上网。

Read 4 Read the paragraph and put a cross (X) in the correct box for each question.

大海是我姐姐的朋友。他的爱好是玩电子游戏，他也喜欢运动，他会打网球，他打得很好。姐姐的爱好是看书和听音乐。他们都喜欢看电影。星期六和星期日他们常常去看电影。

1) Dahai is my .... 's friend.

☐	younger brother
☐	elder brother
☐	elder sister
☐	younger sister

2) Dahai's hobbies are ....

☐	swimming
☐	playing computer games
☐	reading books
☐	doing sports

3) Dahai can play .... very well.

☐	basketball
☐	tennis
☐	football
☐	ping-pong

4) Dahai and my sister often .... on the weekend.

☐	read books
☐	go to the stadium
☐	watch movies
☐	go running

Speak 5 Talk about the pictures in Chinese.

e.g. 她的爱好是听音乐。

Speak
6

Role play. Ask your partner what their hobbies are.

e.g. 你的爱好是什么?

我喜欢看电影和听音乐。

Write
7

Complete the sentences with appropriate Chinese characters.

1) 他喜欢 ☐ ☐ ☐ 。 🎵

2) 我的 ☐ ☐ 是运动。

3) 你喜欢哪个 ☐ ☐ ? 🎥

4) 他的 ☐ ☐ 是 ☐ ☐ ☐ 。

5) 他喜欢这个 ☐ ☐ ，他常常 ☐ 这个 ☐ ☐ 。

Write
8

Translate the following paragraph into English.

我叫京京。我是中国人。我的爱好是看电影和玩电子游戏。我的朋友Jake也喜欢玩电子游戏。星期五下午没有课，我常常和朋友去体育场运动。

Write 9 Translate the following sentences into Chinese.

1）Which book do you like? ....

2）Their hobby is to surf the internet. ....

3）I often drink Chinese tea. ....

Write 10 Practise Chinese characters.

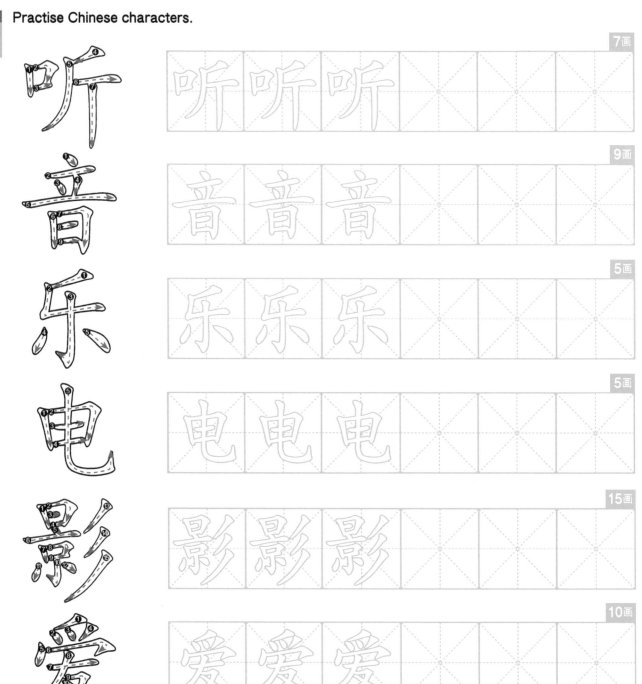

第五单元小结　Unit Five Summary

Months

一月，二月，…… 十一月，十二月	number + 月

Dates

一号，二号，…… 三十号，三十一号	number + 号／日

Order

5月16号，星期五	month – date - day

Asking about dates

你的生日是几月几号？ When is your birthday? 我的生日是一月二十四号 My birthday is 24th January.	someone的生日 ＋ 是 ＋ 几月几号？ someone的生日 ＋ 是 ＋ number月number号
今天是几月几号？ What is the date today? 今天是一月二十四号。 Today is 24th January.	今天 ＋ 是 ＋ 几月几号？ 今天 ＋ 是 ＋ number月number号

Talking about going somewhere (and doing something)

我去图书馆。 I go to the library. 他去体育馆。 He goes to the stadium.	someone + 去 + somewhere
我去看书。 I'm going to read. 姐姐去踢足球。 My elder sister is going to play football.	someone + 去 + verb

Asking 'which' questions

哪个（篮球）好？ Which one (basketball) is better? 这个好。 This one.	哪 + measure word + noun + adjective (description/comment) (When the context is clear, the noun can be dropped)
你喜欢哪本书？ Which book do you like? 我喜欢这本。 I like this one.	someone + 喜欢 + 哪 + measure word + noun

第五单元小结　Unit Five Summary

'this' and 'that'

这本书。 This book. 那个足球。 That football.	这 + measure word + noun 那 + measure word + noun
这是什么？ What is this? 这是足球。 This is a football.	这+是 + 什么？ 这+是 + noun
那是什么？ What is that? 那是网球。 That is a tennis ball.	那+是 + 什么？ 那+是 + noun

Describing how an action is carried out

他跑得很快。 He runs fast. 哥哥游得很好 My elder brother swims well.	someone + verb (action) + 得 + adjective

Talking about what skills you have

我会打乒乓球。 I can play Ping-Pong. 我不会打网球。 I can't play tennis.	someone + 会 + verb (skill) + something someone +不会 + verb (skill) + something

Talking about hobbies

你的爱好是什么？ What is your hobby? 我的爱好是踢足球。 My hobby is playing football.	someone + 的 + 爱好 + 是 + 什么？ someone + 的 + 爱好 + 是 + noun/ verb + noun
他常常喝茶。 He often drinks tea. 我常常看书。 I often read books.	someone + 常常 + verb + noun

第十六课 Lesson

I Go by Plane 我坐飞机去

16

Learning Objectives

交际话题 Topic of conversation:

交通工具 Transport
Jiāotōng gōngjù

基本句型 Sentence patterns:

你怎么去体育馆？　我开车去。
汽车站在前边。

New Words

1　怎么　zěnme　adv. how

2　汽车　qìchē　n. vehicles in general

3　开(车)　kāi (chē)　v. to drive

4　坐　zuò　v. to take or to travel by (a vehicle)

5　公共汽车　gōnggòng qìchē　n. bus

6　汽车站　qìchēzhàn　n. bus station

7　前边　qiánbian　n. / prep. the front; in front of

8　骑　qí　v. to ride

9　自行车/单车　zìxíngchē/dānchē　n. bike, bicycle

10　飞机　fēijī　n. plane

11　火车　huǒchē　n. train

Text

Part I

京京： 大海，你今天去体育馆吗？
Jīngjīng: Dàhǎi, nǐ jīntiān qù tǐyùguǎn ma?

大海： 我去。你呢？
Dàhǎi: Wǒ qù. Nǐ ne?

京京： 我也去。你怎么去体育馆？
Jīngjīng: Wǒ yě qù. Nǐ zěnme qù tǐyùguǎn

大海： 我和哥哥开车去。
Dàhǎi: Wǒ hé gēge kāi chē qù.

京京： 你会开车吗？
Jīngjīng: Nǐ huì kāi chē ma?

大海： 我不会开车，我哥哥会。
Dàhǎi: Wǒ bú huì kāi chē, wǒ gēge huì.

你每天都去体育馆，你怎么去？
Nǐ měi tiān dōu qù tǐyùguǎn, nǐ zěnme qù?

京京： 我坐公共汽车去。
Jīngjīng: Wǒ zuò gōnggòng qìchē qù.

大海： 汽车站在哪儿？
Dàhǎi: Qìchēzhàn zài nǎr?

京京： 汽车站在前边。
Jīngjīng: Qìchēzhàn zài qiánbian.

Jingjing: Dahai, are you going to the gym today?
Dahai: Yes. How about you?
Jingjing: I will go as well. How do you go there?
Dahai: My brother and I go by car.
Jingjing: Can you drive?
Dahai: No, I can't, but my brother can.
　　　　How do you go to the gym every day?
Jingjing: I go by bus.
Dahai: Where is the bus station?
Jingjing: The bus station is ahead.

Part II

我们骑自行车去图书馆

小雨是北京人，她是中学生，是我的同学，也是我的好朋友。我们的爱好都是看书。星期六和星期日，我们没有课，我们常常骑自行车去图书馆，图书馆有我们喜欢的书。小雨今天不去图书馆，她去上海，她坐飞机去上海。七月我也去上海，我坐火车去。

Brain Teaser

Look at the following questions. How is the Chinese sentence order different from English?
汽车站在哪儿? 汽车站在前面。
你怎么去体育馆? 我开车去体育馆。

Grammar Point

1. When talking about travelling in Chinese, simply put the appropriate verb (action) before the mode of transport. Use the following pattern and note the verbs:

Verb + transport

	Verb	Transport
坐	The basic meaning of 坐 is 'to sit'. It is used with any form of transport that you sit inside.	汽车；公共汽车；火车；飞机
开	To ride	车；汽车；公共汽车；火车；飞机
骑	To drive	自行车／单车

2. When saying 'going somewhere by...' in Chinese, we must put the means of transport in front of the action verb 去. See the following pattern:
means of transport + 去
e.g. 他骑自行车去图书馆。
     我坐飞机去法国。

3. 怎么 means 'how'. It is a question word. Like other question words in Chinese, 怎么 takes the same place in the question as where the answer will go.
Someone ＋ 怎么 ＋ 去 ＋ (somewhere).
e.g. 你怎么去体育馆?
     我开车去体育馆。
     你怎么去上海?
     我坐飞机去。

Exercises

 1 Number the following items in the order that they are played in the recording.

Listen 2 Listen to the recording and put a cross (X) in the correct boxes.

1) Where is Lily travelling to?

☐	Beijing
☐	Hong Kong
☐	London
☐	Shanghai

2) Lily is traveling with . . . .

☐	her mother
☐	her father
☐	her elder sister
☐	her younger sister

3) They are travelling by . . . .

☐	plane
☐	train
☐	bike
☐	bus

4) They are not travelling by car because . . . .

☐	they can't drive.
☐	it is too far.
☐	they don't like driving.
☐	they don't have a car.

Read 3 Read the sentence and match it with picture A or B.

他喜欢开车。

弟弟骑自行车去。

 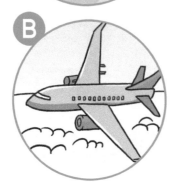

坐火车去伦敦。

那是公共汽车。

他常常坐飞机。

怎么去汽车站？

Read
4

Read the following paragraph and put a cross (X) next to the true sentences.

　　我是小雨，我家在北京，北京很大，我常常坐公共汽车，我也常常骑自行车。现在我是中学生，我们早上八点上课，我喜欢骑自行车去上课。星期六和星期日没有课，我常常和朋友骑自行车去体育馆，我们去打篮球。

Example	His name is Xiaoyu.	×
	Xiaoyu's home is in Beijing.	
	Xiaoyu's home is very big.	
	Xiaoyu often takes the buses.	
	Xiaoyu often takes the train.	
	Xiaoyu likes to go to school by bike	
	Xiaoyu doesn't like going to school by bike.	
	Xiaoyu does not cycle often.	

Speak 5 Talk about the pictures. Where are these people going and what kind of transport do they choose?

e.g. 他怎么去伦敦？他坐飞机去伦敦。

Speak 6 Role play. Find out how your partner goes to school.

e.g. 你怎么去上课？

我坐公共汽车去上课。

Write 7 Complete the sentences with appropriate Chinese characters.

1） 这是 ☐ ☐ ，我喜欢 ☐ ☐ ☐ 。

2） 这是 ☐ ☐ ，爸爸喜欢 ☐ ☐ ☐ 。

3） 你 ☐ 么去上海？我 ☐ 飞机去。

4） 他喜欢骑自行 ☐ ，他骑得很 ☐ 。

5） 你哥哥会开车吗？他 ☐ ☐ ☐ 。

6） 我不喜欢 ☐ 自行车。

Write 8 Translate the following paragraph into English.

> 我和我哥哥都喜欢骑自行车，我骑得不快，哥哥骑得很快。哥哥会开车，我不会。我们也常常坐公共汽车去图书馆和体育馆。七月和八月我们都没有课，我们坐火车去上海，我爸爸朋友的家在上海。

....

....

....

Write 9 Translate the following sentences into Chinese.

1） How are you going to the library?

....

2） He often goes to China by plane.

....

3） My brother and I often play computer games on Saturday.

....

4）The stadium is straight ahead.

Write
10
Practise Chinese characters.

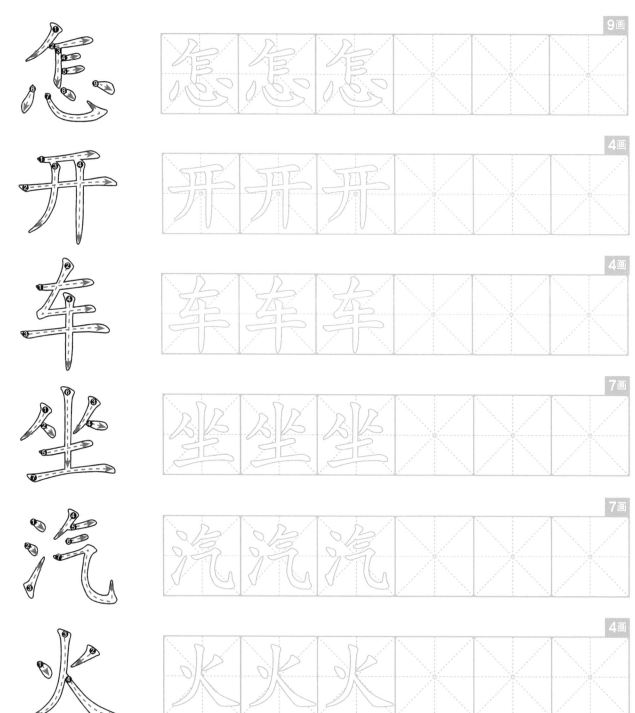

第十七课 Lesson **17**

I'm at the Railway Station 我在火车站

Learning Objectives

交际话题 Topic of conversation:

方向和问路 Directions and Asking
Fāngxiàng hé wènlù for Directions

基本句型 Sentence patterns:

你在哪儿等(我)?　我在家等你。
这是火车站。　那是飞机场。
往右走。

New Words

1. 飞机场 fēijīchǎng **n.** airport
2. 等 děng **v.** to wait for
3. 请问 qǐngwèn Excuse me
4. 走 zǒu **v.** to walk; to go somewhere
5. 火车站 huǒchēzhàn **n.** railway station
6. 往 wǎng **prep.** towards
7. 旁边 pángbiān **n.** the side; next to
8. 后边 hòubian **n.** to the back of; behind
9. 左边 zuǒbian **n.** left side; the left
10. 右边 yòubian **n.** right side; the right

Text

Part I

天天： 玛丽，我们几点去飞机场？
Tiāntiān : Mǎlì, wǒmen jǐ diǎn qù fēijīchǎng ?

玛丽： 十点。我等你。
Mǎlì : Shí diǎn. Wǒ děng nǐ.

天天： 你在哪儿等？
Tiāntiān : Nǐ zài nǎr děng ?

玛丽： 我在家等你，好吗？
Mǎlì : Wǒ zài jiā děng nǐ, hǎo ma ?

天天： 请问，去你家怎么走？
Tiāntiān : Qǐngwèn, qù nǐ jiā zěnme zǒu ?

玛丽： 你现在在哪儿？
Mǎlì : Nǐ xiànzài zài nǎr ?

天天： 我在火车站。
Tiāntiān : Wǒ zài huǒchēzhàn.

玛丽： 我家在图书馆右边，往右走。
Mǎlì : Wǒ jiā zài túshūguǎn yòubian, wǎng yòu zǒu.

天天： 好，我开车去你家。
Tiāntiān : Hǎo, wǒ kāi chē qù nǐ jiā.

玛丽： 我在我家前边等你。
Mǎlì : Wǒ zài wǒ jiā qiánbian děng nǐ.

天天： 好。
Tiāntiān : Hǎo.

Tiantian: When are we going to the airport, Mary?

Mary: At 10 o'clock. I will wait for you.

Tiantian: Where will you be waiting?

Mary: Can I wait for you at home?

Tiantian: Can you tell me how to get to your home, please?

Mary: Where are you now?

Tiantian: I'm at the railway station.

Mary: My home is at the right side of the library.
So turn right there, please.

Tiantian: OK. I will drive to your home.

Mary: I will be waiting in front of my house.

Tiantian: That's fine.

Part II

我家在火车站后边

这是火车站，那是飞机场。我家在火车站后边，我家左边有一个图书馆，右边有一个体育馆。我常常去图书馆和体育馆，我喜欢在图书馆看书，也喜欢在体育馆打乒乓球。飞机场旁边有一个大运动场，我和朋友常常在那个运动场打网球。

Grammar Point

1. We have learned that time phrases, are placed before the verb. It is the same with locations. Remember the following pattern:
   Location phrase + verb
   e.g. 你在哪儿等我？
        我在家等你。
2. When describing locations using a reference point in Chinese, we use the following pattern:
   Reference + direction
   e.g. 图书馆右边
        火车站后边
3. Remember we use 在 to talk about where something is. 在 means 'to be at', so you should not use this word with 是. We also use 有 to talk about location. We use this word to say something exists. It can be translated as 'there is' or 'there are'.
   e.g. 图书馆是在我家左边。（×）
        图书馆在我家旁边。（√）

| 在 | place + 在 + location
e.g. 图书馆在我家左边。 | Emphasises on 'where the place is'. |
| 有 | location + 有 + number + measure word + place
e.g. 我家左边有一个图书馆。 | Emphasises on 'where the place exists'. |

Exercises

Listen
1

Number the following items in the order that they are played in the recording.

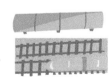

Listen 2 Listen to the recording and answer the following questions in English.

1) Where is the man trying to get to?

....

2) Where is the train station?

....

3) Which way did the woman tell him to go?

....

4) Where have they agreed to meet up later?

....

Read 3 Read the sentence and match it with picture A or B.

请问，飞机场在哪儿？

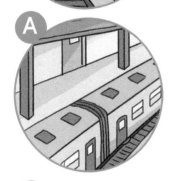

火车站在前边。

往前走。

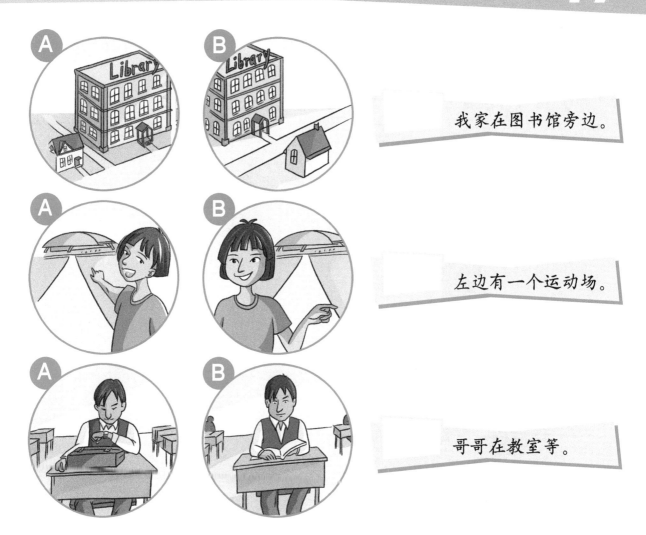

我家在图书馆旁边。

左边有一个运动场。

哥哥在教室等。

Read 4 Read the following paragraph then use the words in the box to complete the translation. There are words that you will not need to use.

今天我和天天坐火车去北京。他家在飞机场旁边，他坐公共汽车去火车站。我家在火车站后边，我骑自行车去。这个火车站很大。火车站右边有汽车站，火车站左边也有汽车站，我在左边的汽车站等天天。

In front of   behind   to the left of   to the right of   next to   bike   train   bus

car   bike

Today Tiantian and I are going to Beijing by .... His home is .... the airport. He goes to the train station by .... My home is .... the train station. I am going there by .... The bus station is .... of the train station. I will wait for Tiantian there.

Speak 5 Describe the following pictures with your partner.

Where are these places?

e.g. 图书馆在哪儿？　图书馆在教室旁边。

Where are you waiting for your friend?

e.g. 你在哪儿等我？　我在家等你。

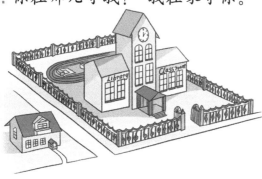 

Speak 6 Role play. Tell your partner what places exist around your house and where they are.

e.g. 你家后边有什么？ 我家后边有火车站。

你家在哪儿？ 我家在体育馆旁边。

Write 7 Complete the sentences with appropriate Chinese characters.

1） 这是 ☐ ☐ 场，那是 ☐ ☐  站。

2） 汽车站在 ☐ 边，往 ☐ 走。

3） 图书馆在我家 ☐ 边，我骑 ☐ ☐ ☐ 去图书馆。

4） 小猫在我 ☐ 边，小狗 ☐ 我 ☐ 边。

5） 运动场 ☐ 图书馆 ☐ 边。

6） 我 ☐ ☐ 等你。

Write 8 Translate the following the dialogue into English.

A: 请问，你们的教室和图书馆在哪儿？

B: 我们的教室在前边，往前走。图书馆在右边。这个图书馆很大，有很多书。我们常常去图书馆。

....

....

A: 你们在哪儿跑步和踢足球？

B: 我们在运动场跑步和踢足球，运动场在图书馆旁边。我们喜欢踢足球，也喜欢跑步。

....

....

Write 9 Translate the following sentences into Chinese.

1） The bus station is on the right side of my house.

....

2）There is a library behind the stadium.

....

3）How do I get to the airport?

....

4）I will wait for you at the classroom.

....

Write
10

Practise Chinese characters.

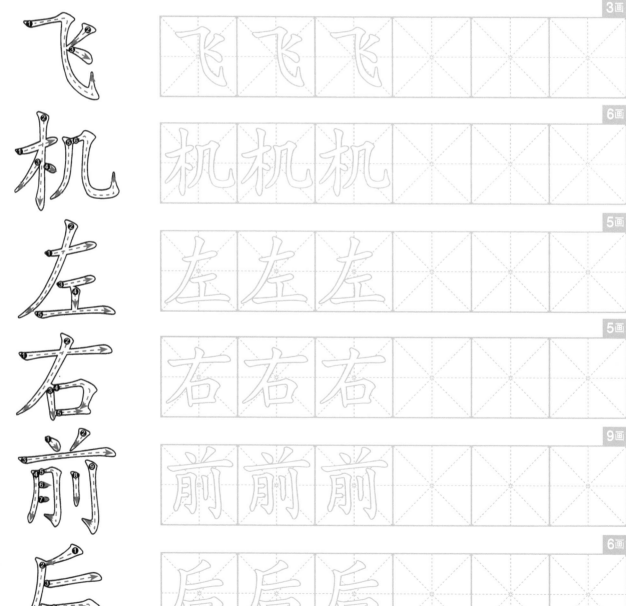

第十八课 Lesson **18**

Today's a Sunny Day　今天是晴天

Learning Objectives

交际话题 Topic of conversation:

天气　Weather
Tiānqì

基本句型 Sentence patterns:

今天天气怎么样？
今天是晴天。
外边没有风。
你冷吗？／你冷不冷？
他冷。／他不冷

New Words

1. 天气　tiānqì　n. weather
2. 怎么样　zěnmeyàng　what about
3. 晴天　qíngtiān　n. sunny day
4. 外边　wàibian　n. outside
5. 风　fēng　n. wind
6. 冷　lěng　adj. cold
7. 热　rè　adj. hot
8. 雨　yǔ　n. rain
9. 下雨　xià yǔ　v. to rain
10. 雪　xuě　n. snow
11. 下雪　xià xuě　v. to snow

Text

Part I

妈妈： 今天天气怎么样？
Māma： Jīntiān tiānqì zěnmeyàng?

爸爸： 今天晴天，不下雪。
Bàba： Jīntiān qíngtiān, bú xià xuě.

妈妈： 我们和大海去运动场，好吗？
Māma： Wǒmen hé Dàhǎi qù yùndòngchǎng, hǎo ma?

爸爸： 好，我们怎么去？
Bàba： Hǎo, wǒmen zěnme qù?

妈妈： 骑自行车去。
Māma： Qí zìxíngchē qù.

爸爸： 外边有风吗？
Bàba： Wàibian yǒu fēng ma?

妈妈： 外边没有风。
Māma： Wàibian méiyǒu fēng.

爸爸： 好，我们骑自行车去。
Bàba： Hǎo, wǒmen qí zìxíngchē qù.

Mum: What's the weather like today?
Dad: Today's a sunny day, it doesn't snow.
Mum: How about we go to the stadium with Dahai?
Dad: OK. How do we go?
Mum: By bicycle.
Dad: Is it windy outside?
Mum: It's not windy outside.
Dad: Great. Let's ride.
Mum: Are you cold?
Dad: I'm not cold. The weather is nice today. Are you cold?
Mum: I'm not cold, either. I like riding a bicycle on a sunny day.
Dad: Is Dahai cold?
Mum: He rides very fast. He isn't cold.
Dad: True, he isn't cold.

妈妈： 你冷吗？
Māma： Nǐ lěng ma?

爸爸： 我不冷，今天天气很好。你冷不冷？
Bàba： Wǒ bù lěng, jīntiān tiānqì hěn hǎo. Nǐ lěng bù lěng?

妈妈： 我也不冷。我喜欢晴天骑自行车。
Māma： Wǒ yě bù lěng. Wǒ xǐhuan qíngtiān qí zìxíngchē.

爸爸： 大海冷吗？
Bàba： Dàhǎi lěng ma?

妈妈： 他骑得很快，他不冷。
Māma： Tā qí de hěn kuài, tā bù lěng.

爸爸： 是，他不会冷。
Bàba： Shì, tā bú huì lěng.

Part II

To: Tiantian@gmail.com

Add Cc | Add Bcc

Subject: 上午晴天，下午下雨

Attach a file   Insert: Invitation   Check Spelling ▼

B *I* U F· T· T· T· ∞ & := := ⫶ ⫶ " ▤ ▤ ▤ T· « Plain Text

天天：

　　你好！

　　上海怎么样？天气好吗？热不热？今天是星期六，我没有课。上午是晴天，外边没有风，我和爸爸妈妈骑自行车去运动场，我们打网球。中午天气很热，我们去体育馆游泳。下午下雨，雨很大，我们都在家，我玩电子游戏，爸爸读书，妈妈听音乐。我喜欢星期六。

　　　　　　　　　　　　　　　　　　　　　　大卫

　　　　　　　　　　　　　　　　　　　　　　6月29日

Send   Save Now   Discard

Grammar Point

1. 怎么样 is an interrogative (a question word). It can be translated as 'how about...' or 'What is (something) like'. When asking about the topic or subject, such as, weather, food, feeling and etc., we can use the following basic pattern:
   Subject + 怎么样?
   e.g. 今天天气怎么样?
   　　 这个红苹果怎么样?

2. We know that we can add 吗 to the end of a statement to turn it into a yes/no question. Another way of asking yes/no questions is the affirmative-negative question. The affirmative form is always paced before the negative.
   e.g. 你冷不冷?
   　　 她喜欢不喜欢小猫?

   NOTE when using affirmative-negative questions to talk about existence or ownership, always use 有没有.
   e.g. 外边有没有风? (√)
   　　 外边有不有风? (✕)

Exercises

Listen 1 Number the following items in the order that they are played in the recording.

Listen 2 Listen to the recording and complete the gaps in each sentence using a word from the box below. There are more words than gaps.

Friday   Saturday   Sunday   windy   sunny   rainy   not cold   not windy   cold

windy   go swimming   do sports   ride bikes   Chinese bread   Chinese noodles

Today is .... The weather is .... and the temperature outside is

.... My parents and I are going to .... We are going to have

.... for lunch. We all really like it!

Read 3 Read the sentence and match it with picture A or B.

今天是晴天。

星期五下雨。

外边没有风。

星期三下雪。

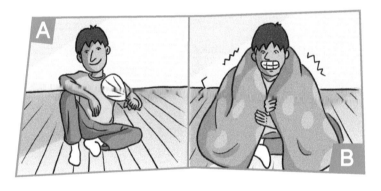

我不冷。

天气怎么样?

你热不热?

Read 4 Read the paragraph below and put a cross (X) in the correct box for each question.

> 大海家在北京，他喜欢北京的天气。今天是晴天，外边没有风，很热。下午没有课，大海和京京骑自行车去体育馆，他们去游泳。大海喜欢游泳，京京也喜欢游泳，他们都游得很快。

1) Dahai likes Beijing's ....

☐	people
☐	noodles
☐	weather
☐	rice

2) Today's weather is ....

☐	rainy
☐	windy
☐	snowy
☐	sunny

3) It is .... and .... outside.

☐	snowy
☐	not windy
☐	rainy
☐	cold
☐	hot

4) Dahai and Jingjing are going to the stadium by ....

☐	bus
☐	car
☐	bike
☐	train

Speak 5 Talk about the pictures below. Describe the weather of each of the days in Chinese.

e.g. 星期一下雨。

Speak 6 Role play. Ask your partner about the weather today, yesterday ^{zuó tiān}（昨天） and tomorrow ^{míng tiān}（明天）.

e.g. 今天天气怎么样？

今天下雨。

Write
7

Complete the sentences with appropriate Chinese characters.

1）今天 ☐ ☐ 怎么样？

2）今天是 ☐ ☐ ，明天有 ☐ 。

3）外边 ☐ ☐ ，很 ☐ 。

4）今天没有 ☐ ，没有 ☐ ，很 ☐ 。

5）外边风很大，你 ☐ ☐ ☐ ？

6）你有 ☐ ☐ 小狗？

Write
8

Translate the following the dialogue into English.

我和爸爸都喜欢运动。我们常常去踢足球。我们都踢得很好。今天是星期天，上午天气很好。外面有风，不热。我们上午开车去运动场踢足球。中午天气很热，我们在图书馆看书。晚上天气很冷，我们在家吃晚饭 (dinner)。我爸爸喜欢喝咖啡，我喜欢喝果汁。我们都喜欢吃牛肉和青菜。

....

....

....

Write 9 Translate the following sentences into Chinese.

1） It's windy outside.

2） How is the weather today?

3） It was rainy and snowy yesterday. It was very cold.

4） I like riding the bicycle on a sunny day with my dad.

Write 10 Practise Chinese characters.

4画

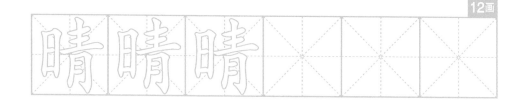
12画

4画

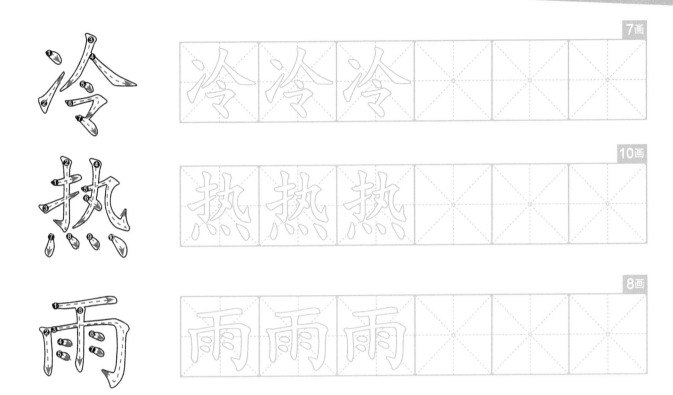

7画

10画

8画

Modern Transport in China

A bicycle-sharing system, or bike-share scheme, is a service that makes bicycles available to individuals for shared use on a short-term basis. Bike-share schemes allow people to borrow a bike from point A and return it at point B. For many systems, smartphone mapping apps show nearby stations with available bikes and open docks.

These programs are very popular, inexpensive, promote health, and reduce dependence on fossil fuels. The Chinese government wants 18 percent of commuters to use bikes by 2020. Hangzhou's program is the most successful: more than 30 percent of the city's commuters rely on bike-sharing. In Beijing, bike-sharing has been central to the city's efforts in reducing pollution.

High-speed rail

In today's connected world, transportation between cities is equally as important as that within cities. High-speed rail (HSR) systems can help, by covering distances that are too great for city buses or metro lines, but too near to require the hassle of air travel. China currently has the world's largest HSR system, with more than 19,000 km of railways connecting 28 of China's 33 provinces. The system had 2.5 million daily riders in 2014, a ten-fold increase since 2007. The Shanghai Maglev line is the first commercial HSR to use 'magnetic levitation' to reach speeds of more than 400 km/h.

第六单元小结　Unit Six Summary

Going somewhere by different forms of transport

你怎么去体育馆？ How are you going to the stadium? 你怎么去上海？ How are you going to Shanghai?	Someone + 怎么 + 去 + somewhere
我坐公共汽车去体育馆。 I am going to the stadium by bus. 我开车去上海。 I am going to Shanghai by car.	Someone + verb + transport + 去 + somewhere

Describing location

图书馆右边 right side of the library 火车站后边 backside of the railway station (behind)	Reference + direction
图书馆在我家左边。 The library is on the left of my house. 我家左边有一个图书馆。 There is a library on the left of my house.	Place + 在 + location Location + 有 + number + measure word + place

Describing doing something at somewhere

你在哪儿等我？ Where are you waiting for me?	在 + 哪儿 + verb
我在家等你。 I will wait for you at home.	在 + location + verb

Asking and giving directions

去你家怎么走？ How do I get to your home? 去图书馆怎么走？ How do I get to the library?	去 + destination + 怎么走？
往前走。 Go straight. 往左开。 Drive towards the left.	往 + direction + verb（走 or 开）

第六单元小结　Unit Six Summary

Talking about the weather （topic + comment）

今天天气怎么样？ How/what is the weather today? 外面天气怎么样？ How/what is the weather outside?	……天气 + 怎么样？ topic
今天晴天。Today is sunny. 今天不下雨　Today is not raining. 外面有风。　Outside is windy. 外面没有风。Outside is not windy.	Topic + weather

Asking 'yes/no' questions

你冷吗？ Are you cold? 你去图书馆吗？ Are you going to the library?	Statement + 吗？
你冷不冷？ Are you cold? 你去不去图书馆？ Are you going to the library?	Adjective + 不 + adjective Verb + 不 + verb
你有猫吗？ 你有没有猫？ Do you have cats?	有 – 没有　（not*不有）

第十九课 Lesson

19

He Likes Pop Music 他喜欢流行音乐

Learning Objectives

交际话题 Topic of conversation:

音乐会 Concerts
Yīnyuèhuì

基本句型 Sentence patterns:

他喜欢流行音乐。　音乐会人很多。
古典音乐很好听。　他对流行音乐很有兴趣。

New Words

1 对 duì **prep.** to, for
2 兴趣 xìngqù **n.** interest
3 表演 biǎoyǎn **n.** performance
4 音乐会 yīnyuèhuì **n.** concert
5 了 le **part.** used after verbs (action words) to indicate an action is completed

6 流行 liúxíng **adj.** popular
7 古典 gǔdiǎn **adj.** classical
8 回来 huílái **v.** to return, to come back
9 好听 hǎotīng **adj.** pleasing to the ear
10 见 jiàn **v.** to see
11 多 duō **adj.** many, how (+adj.)

Text

Part I

（本和小雨放学后）
Běn hé Xiǎoyǔ fàng xué hòu

本：　今天下午你去我家玩，好吗？
Běn:　Jīntiān xiàwǔ nǐ qù wǒ jiā wán, hǎo ma?

小雨：　好，下午见。
Xiǎoyǔ:　Hǎo, xiàwǔ jiàn.

(After school)
Ben: Can you come to my home this afternoon, please?
Xiaoyu: Yes. See you this afternoon.

（在本家）
Zài Běn jiā

小雨：　你爸爸妈妈不在家吗？
Xiǎoyǔ:　Nǐ bàba māma bú zài jiā ma?

本：　不在家，今天他们去音乐会了。
Běn:　Bú zài jiā, jīntiān tāmen qù yīnyuèhuì le.

小雨：　你哥哥没去吗？
Xiǎoyǔ:　Nǐ gēge méi qù ma?

本：　那是古典音乐会，他不喜欢古典音乐。
Běn:　Nà shì gǔdiǎn yīnyuèhuì, tā bù xǐhuan gǔdiǎn yīnyuè.

小雨：　他喜欢什么音乐？
Xiǎoyǔ:　Tā xǐhuan shénme yīnyuè?

本：　哥哥喜欢流行音乐。
Běn:　Gēge xǐhuan liúxíng yīnyuè.

(At Ben's home)
Xiaoyu: Aren't your parents at home?
Ben: They are not at home. They went to a concert today.
Xiaoyu: Did your elder brother go as well?
Ben: That is a classical concert. My elder brother doesn't like classical music.
Xiaoyu: What music does he like?
Ben: He likes pop music.

（晚上本的爸爸妈妈回来后）
Wǎnshang Běn de bàba māma huílái hòu

本： 音乐会怎么样？
Běn: Yīnyuèhuì zěnme yàng?

爸爸： 很好，音乐会人很多。
Bàba: Hěn hǎo, yīnyuèhuì rén hěn duō.

本： 妈妈，你喜欢这个音乐会吗？
Běn: Māma, nǐ xǐhuan zhège yīnyuèhuì ma?

妈妈： 我很喜欢，古典音乐很好听。
Māma: Wǒ hěn xǐhuan, gǔdiǎn yīnyuè hěn hǎotīng.

Learning Tip

A good way of developing your speaking and writing is to avoid repetition. When talking about likes or dislikes in Chinese, you can use 喜欢 or 爱 (to love). BUT remember you can also use 对......（很）有兴趣。

(Ben's parents came back from the concert in the evening.)
Ben: How about the concert?
Dad: Very good. There were many people at the concert.
Ben: Did you like the concert, Mum?
Mum: I liked it very much. Classical music is pleasing to the ear.

Part II

他对流行音乐很有兴趣

我家的人都喜欢音乐。我爸爸妈妈喜欢古典音乐，他们常常去听古典音乐，他们有很多古典音乐的CD。我哥哥不喜欢古典音乐，他对流行音乐很有兴趣。他有很多流行音乐的CD，他每天都听。他也常常和朋友去看流行音乐表演。我也喜欢流行音乐，流行音乐很好听。

Grammar Point

1. 了 is a useful particle. It shows that a verb (action) is completed. 了 is placed after the verb or, in simple sentences, it is placed at the end of the sentence.
For example: 他们去音乐会了。
了 can also show a new situation. In this case, 了 always comes at the end.
For example: 现在上课了。
(they were not in class, but they now are.)
图书馆开门了。
(The library has opened, but it was not open before)

2. To become interested in an activity or subject, or start being involved in an activity. Use the following pattern:
Someone + 对 + ... + （很）有兴趣
e.g. 他对流行音乐有兴趣。
哥哥对足球很有兴趣。

3. 好 can be put in front of many verbs (actions) to form adjectives.
e.g. 好吃 (delicious); 好听 (pleasant to the ear); 好看 (nice looking; pretty)

Exercises

Listen 1 Number the following items in the order that they are played in the recording.

Listen 2 Listen to the recording and put a cross (X) in the correct box.

1) Who is interested in classical music?

☐	Just me
☐	My younger brother and I
☐	My elder brother and I
☐	None of us

2) Who is interested in pop music?

☐	Just me
☐	My younger brother and I
☐	My elder brother and I
☐	None of us

3) Who thinks Taylor Swift's music is great?

☐	Just me
☐	My younger brother
☐	My elder brother
☐	Both of us

4) Who often goes to One Direction concerts?

☐	Just me
☐	My younger brother
☐	My elder brother
☐	Both of us

Read 3 Read the sentence and match it with picture A or B.

音乐会人很多。

音乐会人不多。

这个音乐很好听。

那个电影很好看。

这个菜不好吃。

那个汽水不好喝。

Read
4　Read the following paragraph and put a cross (X) next to the true statements.

> 　　我喜欢流行音乐，流行音乐很好听。我有很多流行音乐的CD，我也常常看流行音乐表演。我不喜欢古典音乐，对古典音乐没有兴趣。哥哥也不喜欢古典音乐，他对流行音乐很有兴趣。

Example	I am interested in music.	×
	I like classical music.	
	I think pop music is nice.	
	I have a lot of classical music CDs.	
	I have a lot of pop music CDs.	
	My brother likes classical music.	
	My bother likes pop music.	
	My brother is interested in classical music.	

Speak
5　Answer the questions in Chinese according to the pictures.

● 爸爸妈妈喜欢什么音乐？
● 他们常常去哪儿？

● 哥哥对什么音乐有兴趣？
● 他常常去哪儿？

● 妹妹喜欢古典音乐吗？
● 她怎么听喜欢的音乐？

● 姐姐喜欢听流行音乐吗？

Speak
6　Role play. Find out what kind of music your partner and his/her family members like.

e.g. 你喜欢什么音乐？ ／ 你妈妈喜欢什么音乐？

我喜欢流行音乐。 ／ 她喜欢古典音乐。

Write 7 Complete the sentences with appropriate Chinese characters.

1) 你对 ☐ ☐ 音乐有兴趣？

2) 你对古典音乐有 ☐ ☐ 吗？

3) 我不喜欢古典音乐，我对 ☐ ☐ 音乐有兴趣。

4) 这个音乐很 ☐ ☐ 。

5) 爸爸妈妈去听古典 ☐ ☐ ，我不去。

6) 我 ☐ 古典音乐很有兴趣。

Write 8 Translate the following sentences into English.

1) 你妹妹对什么音乐感兴趣？

．．．

2) 我和朋友们常常去看流行音乐表演。

．．．

3) 我姐姐不喜欢看古典音乐会。

．．．

4) 音乐会人很多。

．．．

Write
9

Translate the text below into Chinese.

My elder sister is very interested in pop music. She likes Justin Bieber. She has a lot of his music CDs. My elder sister went to Justin Bieber's concert yesterday.

....

....

....

Write
10

Practise Chinese characters.

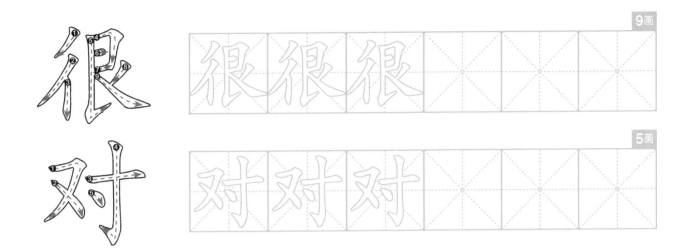

9画

5画

Chinese Celebrities

Yao Ming is a Chinese basketball player who became an international star as a center for the NBA team, the Houston Rockets.

Yao was born to accomplished basketball-playing parents who were both over 6 feet (1.8 meters) tall. In 1997, he joined the Chinese Basketball Association's (CBA's) Shanghai Sharks. By the time he led the Chinese Olympic basketball team to a respectable 10th-place at the 2000 Olympic Games in Sydney, Yao had already become a national icon. He was drafted by the Houston Rockets as the first pick in the 2002 NBA draft. That season, he was an All-Star and was on the leagues All-Rookie team — an honour given to top rookies during the regular season. Over the following six seasons, Yao earned all-star honours and helped the Rockets to playoff appearances in five of those years. Yao soon became the focus of the NBA's efforts to popularise the league around

the globe.

Yao's impact on basketball culture extended far past his on-court accomplishments. He drew large crowds wherever the Rockets played, and their games were broadcast to huge audiences in China and other Asian countries.

第二十课 Lesson

20

He Is Watching the News 他在看新闻

Learning Objectives

交际话题 Topic of conversation:

电视节目 TV Programmes
Diànshì jiémù

基本句型 Sentence patterns:

这个节目很好看。 足球比赛开始了。 他在看新闻。

New Words

1 电视 diànshì n. TV (programme)

2 电视机 diànshìjī n. TV set

3 节目 jiémù n. programme

4 比赛 bǐsài n. match, competition

5 开始 kāishǐ v. to begin

6 新闻 xīnwén n. news

7 (正)在 (zhèng)zài adv. be doing sth.

8 预报 yùbào n. (weather) forecast

Text

Part I

弟弟： 你在看什么节目？
Dìdi： Nǐ zài kàn shénme jiémù？

天天： 我在看流行音乐表演。
Tiāntiān： Wǒ zài kàn liúxíng yīnyuè biǎoyǎn.

弟弟： 这个节目怎么样？
Dìdi： Zhège jiémù zěnmeyàng？

天天： 这个节目很好看，表演很好。
Tiāntiān： Zhège jiémù hěn hǎokàn, biǎoyǎn hěn hǎo.

弟弟： 足球比赛开始了，我看足球比赛，好吗？
Dìdi： Zúqiú bǐsài kāishǐ le, wǒ kàn zúqiú bǐsài, hǎo ma？

天天： 你去爸爸的房间看足球比赛。
Tiāntiān： Nǐ qù bàba de fángjiān kàn zúqiú bǐsài.

弟弟： 爸爸没有看电视吗？
Dìdi： Bàba méiyǒu kàn diànshì ma？

天天： 没有，他去打网球了。
Tiāntiān： Méiyǒu, tā qù dǎ wǎngqiú le.

Learning Tip

When forming a negative sentence, 不 is used to talk about now, the future, and when you do not do something as a habit. When talking about the past, you should negate verbs with 没(有).

Younger brother: What programme are you watching?
Tiantian: I'm watching the pop music show.
Younger brother: How about this programme?
Tiantian: This programme is great.
　　　　　The performance is very good.
Younger brother: The football match is beginning now.
　　　　　Can I watch the match?
Tiantian: You can go and watch it in dad's room.
Younger brother: Wasn't he watching TV?
Tiantian: No, he went to play tennis.

妹妹：爸爸在看什么节目？
Mèimei:　Bàba zài kàn shénme jiémù?

小雨：他在看新闻。
Xiǎoyǔ:　Tā zài kàn xīnwén.

妹妹：他常 常 看新闻，新闻好看吗？
Mèimei:　Tā chángcháng kàn xīnwén,　xīnwén hǎokàn ma?

小雨：爸爸喜欢，我不喜欢新闻节目。
Xiǎoyǔ:　Bàba xǐhuan,　wǒ bù xǐhuan xīnwén jiémù.

Younger sister: What programme is dad watching?
Xiaoyu: He is watching the news.
Younger sister: He often watches the news.
　　　　　Is that interesting?
Xiaoyu: Dad likes it. I don't like watching the news.

Part II

我家有两个电视机

　　我家有两个电视机。爸爸不喜欢看电视，对电视节目没有兴趣，他喜欢听音乐。妈妈喜欢看电视，她喜欢看新闻节目，也喜欢看电影。现在她正在看一个中国电影。我和弟弟都对运动很有兴趣，喜欢看运动节目，弟弟喜欢看篮球比赛，我喜欢看网球节目。现在我们正在看一个足球比赛。

Grammar Point

1. 没有 is the negative form of 有。没有 can be used to negate past actions (to say that someone didn't do something, or something didn't happen). See the following pattern:
   Someone/something + 没有 + verb (action)
   e.g. 比赛没有开始。
   　　爸爸没有去打网球。
   　　我没有吃早饭。

2. When describing an action that is in progress, put (正)在 before the verb (action) to show that it is ongoing. Remember the following pattern:
   e.g. 我（正）在看电视。
   　　他们（正）在上汉语课。

Exercises

Listen 1 Number the following items in the order that they are played in the recording.

Listen 2 Listen to the recording and answer the following questions in English.

1) What is the woman watching?

....

2) Is he going to join her? Why?

....

3) What is he doing now?

....

Read 3 Read the sentence and match it with picture A or B.

新闻节目开始了。

这个比赛很好看。

表演没有开始。

妈妈在看电影。

爸爸不看电视节目。

他没在看电视。

Read 4 Read the following paragraph then use the words in the box to complete the translation. There are words that you will not need to use.

我的朋友都喜欢看电视。Mingming喜欢看新闻，他常常看新闻节目。Dingding对运动有兴趣，他喜欢看比赛，足球比赛、篮球比赛、网球比赛，他都喜欢看。Lanlan喜欢流行音乐，她常常看表演。丽丽呢？她正在看天气预报。我正在看一个法国电影。

| Swimming | football | running | tennis | basketball | Mingming | Lanlan | I |

| Lili (丽丽) | Chinese movie | French movie | British movie |

We all like to watch TV. Dingding likes to watch .... , ... and ....

.... matches. .... like(s) to watch news. .... like(s) pop music.

.... is watching the weather report. I am watching a ....

Speak 5 Answer the questions in Chinese according to the pictures.

● 爸爸妈妈喜欢看什么电视节目？   ● 姐姐在看什么节目？

● 哥哥对什么节目有兴趣？   ● 谁喜欢看足球比赛？

Speak
6

Role play. Find out what kind of TV programs your partner and his/her family members like to watch.

e.g. 你喜欢什么电视节目？　/　你妈妈喜欢什么电视节目？

我喜欢足球比赛。　/　她喜欢法国电影。

Write
7

Complete the sentences with appropriate Chinese characters.

1）你喜欢看 ☐ ☐ 吗?

2）你喜欢看什么电视 ☐ ☐ ?

3）今天有足球 ☐ ☐ 。

4）新闻 ☐ ☐ 了吗?

5）妈妈 ☐ 看电影，我也去看。

6）电影开始 ☐ （started）。

7）我今天 ☐ ☐ 看电视。　（did not watch TV）

Write
8

Translate the sentences into English.

1）流行音乐会开始了。

2）现在是星期天上午十点，我们在吃早饭。

....

3）今天上午有足球比赛，我没有看新闻。

....

4）现在没有课，我和朋友们在玩电子游戏。

....

Write 9 Translate the following paragraph into Chinese.

> I like to watch TV. I am interested in music programs. My friends and I often watch music programs. It is 5 pm now. I am reading books. There will be music programs tonight. They start at 7 pm.

....

....

....

Write 10 Practise Chinese characters.

8画

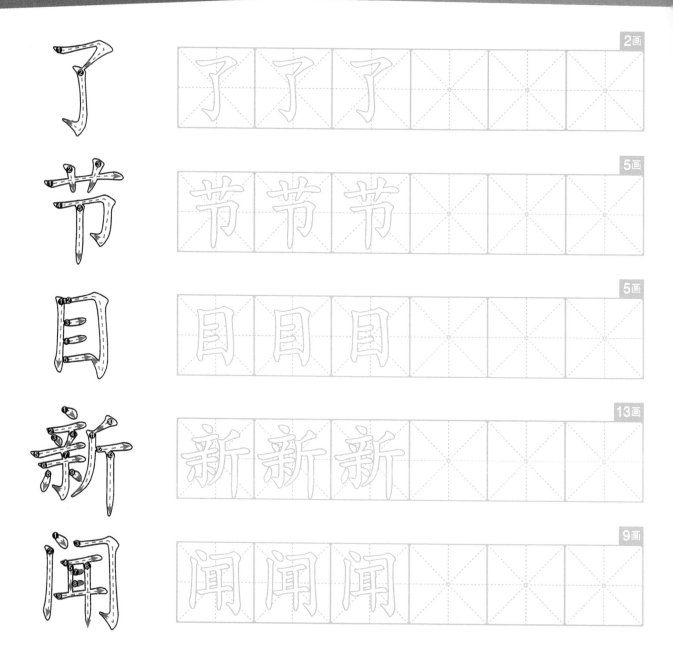

第二十一课 Lesson

21

这个电影很有意思
This Movie Is Very Interesting

Learning Objectives

交际话题 Topic of conversation:

电影 Movie
Diàn yǐng

基本句型 Sentence patterns:

有什么电影？　这个电影很有意思。
我喜欢看电影。　我看了很多他的电影。

New Words

1. 有意思　yǒu yìsi　adj. interesting
2. 没意思　méi yìsi　adj. boring
3. 演员　yǎnyuán　n. actor/actress
4. 有名　yǒumíng　adj. famous
5. 晚上　wǎnshang　n. evening
6. 周末　zhōumò　n. weekend
7. 知道　zhīdào　v. to know
8. 最　zuì　adv. most

Text

Part I

大海：你上网了吗？
Dàhǎi：Nǐ shàng wǎng le ma？

京京：我上网了。
Jīngjīng：Wǒ shàng wǎng le.

大海：今天有什么电影？
Dàhǎi：Jīntiān yǒu shénme diànyǐng？

京京：有一个美国电影。
Jīngjīng：Yǒu yí gè Měiguó diànyǐng.

大海：这个电影有意思吗？
Dàhǎi：Zhège diànyǐng yǒu yìsi ma？

京京：很有意思。
Jīngjīng：Hěn yǒu yìsi.

大海：几点开始？
Dàhǎi：Jǐ diǎn kāishǐ？

京京：下午三点。
Jīngjīng：Xiàwǔ sān diǎn.

大海：下午我们去看这个电影，好吗？
Dàhǎi：Xiàwǔ wǒmen qù kàn zhège diànyǐng, hǎo ma？

京京：好。
Jīngjīng：Hǎo.

大海：我们怎么去？
Dàhǎi：Wǒmen zěnme qù？

京京：骑自行车去。
Jīngjīng：Qí zìxíngchē qù.

大海：我在图书馆前边等你。
Dàhǎi：Wǒ zài túshūguǎn qiánbian děng nǐ.

京京：我们几点见？
Jīngjīng：Wǒmen jǐ diǎn jiàn？

大海：两点半怎么样？
Dàhǎi：Liǎng diǎn bàn zěnmeyàng？

京京：好，两点半见。
Jīngjīng：Hǎo, Liǎng diǎn bàn jiàn.

Dahai: Have you logged on to the Internet?
Jingjing: Yes, I have.
Dahai: What movie is on today?
Jingjing: There is an American movie.
Dahai: Is the movie interesting?
Jingjing: It's very interesting.
Dahai: When is it going to start?
Jingjing: At three o'clock in the afternoon.
Dahai: Shall we go watch this movie?
Jingjing: All right.
Dahai: How will we go?
Jingjing: By bicycle.
Dahai: I will be waiting for you in front of the library.
Jingjing: When shall we meet?
Dahai: How about 2:30?
Jingjing: OK. See you at 2:30.

Learning Tip

Superlatives are the best! In English we form the superlative by adding 'most' before or '-est' after an adjective: e.g. most interesting, most boring, or biggest and smallest. In Chinese making the superlative adjective is simpler, just add 最 before an adjective. Look at the adjectives（大、小、冷、热）we have learned so far and pair them with 最.

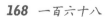

我喜欢看电影

　　我喜欢看电影，美国电影、法国电影、中国电影我都喜欢看，我也知道很多有名的演员。我最喜欢Brad Pitt，他表演得很好，他的电影都很有意思，我看了很多他的电影。周末我去看电影了，那个电影我不喜欢，没意思。星期二有Brad Pitt的电影，晚上七点半开始。我和弟弟都去。

Mr. & Mrs. Smith

Grammar Point

1. Using 最 is the most common way to form a superlative (best, worst, biggest, smallest, etc.) in Chinese. 最 can be added before an adjective and a few psychological verbs.

最 + psychological verbs
The pattern above is to express what one 'most likes' or 'most hates'. This is a great way to talk

about what one likes the most.
e.g. 我最喜欢中国菜！
姐姐最喜欢什么颜色？

最 + adjective
e.g. 这只猫最小。
这个节目最有意思。

Exercises

Listen to the recording and put a cross (X) in the correct boxes.

1)　☐ This actor is very famous.

☐ This actor is not famous.

2)　☐ I know this movie.

☐ I don't know this movie.

3)　☐ I like that British actor most.

☐ I like that American actor most.

4)　☐ Today's movie is interesting.

☐ Today's movie is not interesting.

Listen to the recording and complete the sentences by choosing a word or words from the box. There are words that you will not need to use.

British movie　Chinese movie　American movie　classmates　friends　interesting

boring　7:00　7:15　7:30　bike　bus

I like .... the most. I am going to watch Spiderman with my .... I think

the film will be .... The film starts at .... I am going to get there by ....

....

Read the sentence and match it with picture A or B.

今天有什么电影？

那个节目有意思吗?

这个表演很有意思。

我最喜欢Peter的电影。

Maggie是最有名的演员。

那个比赛很没意思。

Read
4　Read the paragraph and put a cross (X) in the correct box for each question.

　　我喜欢看中国电影，我知道Zhang Ziyi，她是很有名的演员，表演得很好，她的电影都很有意思，我看了很多她的电影。这个周末，晚上的电视有她的节目，九点一刻开始，我在家看她的电影。

1) I like to watch .... films.

☐	French
☐	American
☐	British
☐	Chinese

2) Zhang Ziyi is ....

☐	a famous actress
☐	my friend
☐	my mother
☐	my sister

3) Zhang Ziyi's movie will be on TV ....

☐	this evening
☐	this afternoon
☐	in evening of this weekend
☐	in the afternoon of this weekend

4) Zhangziyi's movie starts at ....

☐	9:30
☐	9:15
☐	6:00
☐	6:30

Speak
5　Talk about the following topics in Chinese. Bring a picture of a movie or an actor/actress and make a brief introduction. You can use the sentences below.

这是一个中国演员，他／她叫……

我知道他／她的电影。

这是现在美国最有名的电影。

这个电影很有意思。

……表演得很好。

Speak
6　Role play. Tell your partner about your favourite film and favourite actor/actress.

> **e.g.** 我最喜欢的电影是Transformers.
>
> 我最喜欢的演员是Brad Pitt.

Write 7 Complete the sentences with appropriate Chinese characters.

1）我不 ☐ ☐ 他是谁。

2）这是英国最 ☐ ☐ ☐ 的节目。

3）他是一个电影 ☐ ☐ 。

4）今天 ☐ ☐ 有比赛(evening) 。

5）☐ ☐ 天气很好，我们去打篮球，好吗(weekend)？

Write 8 Translate the sentences into English.

1）我知道很多有名的电影演员。

....

2）周末我去看电影了，电影很有意思。

....

3）我最喜欢吃红色的苹果。

....

4）我今天有课，没有上网。

....

Write 9 Translate the following paragraph into Chinese.

> I like sports. Football, tennis, ping-pong, basketball, I like them all. I like football the most. I can play football very well. I also like watching football matches. I watched a match this weekend, it was interesting.

....

....

....

....

Write 9 Practise Chinese characters.

意 意 意 意　13画

思 思 思 思　9画

晚 晚 晚 晚　11画

知 知 知 知　8画

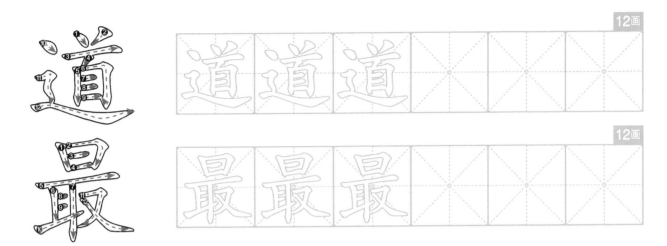

12画

12画

Chinese Celebrities

Zhang Ziyi is a very famous Chinese actress and one of the most well-known Asian actresses in the West. She was born on February 9, 1979, in Beijing, China. As a child, she pursued her interests in dance and gymnastics. At the age of 19, Zhang Ziyi auditioned for a shampoo commercial, which was being made by famed director Zhang Yimou. Little did Zhang Ziyi know, the famed director was using the advertisement as a way to screen actresses for his upcoming film, The Road Home. He chose Zhang Ziyi for the lead role of a young girl who falls in love with a teacher assigned to work in the country village where she lives. Zhang Ziyi became famous in China after this film.

In 2000, Zhang landed a high-profile part as the headstrong Jen Yu in Ang Lee's film, Crouching Tiger, Hidden Dragon. The movie was an enormous success in China and across the world, and earned Zhang Ziyi the

award for Best Supporting actress at both the Independent Spirit and Toronto Film Critics festivals.

Later on, Zhang Ziyi won the Golden Globe Award for Best Actress for her role in Memoirs of a Geisha.

第七单元小结　Unit Seven Summary

Talking about interests

他对流行音乐很有兴趣。 He is very interested in pop music. 我对足球有兴趣。 I am interested in football.	Someone + 对 + …. + （很）有兴趣
他喜欢流行音乐。He likes pop music. 老师喜欢中国电影。The teacher likes Chinese movies.	Someone + 喜欢 + something

Giving compliments

好看 nice to watch / nice to look at (pretty) 好听 nice to listen to	好 + verb
古典音乐很好听。Classical music is pleasant. 这个节目很好看。This programme is good.	Topic + comment Something/someone +很+ 好+verb

Talking about things that happened in the past

比赛开始了。The match has begun. 他去打网球了。He has gone to play tennis.	Someone/something + verb(action) + 了
比赛没有开始。The match hasn't begun. 他没有去打网球。He hasn't gone to play tennis.	Someone/something + 没有 + verb (action)
我看了很多他的电影。 I watched many of his movies. 他看了很多中文书。 He read many Chinese books.	Someone + verb + 了 + something

没有 vs 不

我不吃面条。I don't eat noodles. 今天我不吃面条。Today I will not eat noodles.	不 is used for the present and future
昨天我没有吃面条。 Yesterday I didn't eat noodles.	没有 is used for the past

Talking about an action that is happening

我（正）在看电视。I am watching TV. 他（正）在看什么节目？ What programme is he watching?	Someone + (正)在 + verb (action) + something

Expressing opinions

这个电影很有意思。This movie is interesting. 那本书很没意思。That book is boring.	Topic + comment something/someone + 很 + 有意思 something/someone + 很 + 没意思
你冷不冷？Are you cold? 你去不去图书馆？Are you going to the library?	Adjective + 不 + adjective Verb + 不 + verb

第二十二课 Lesson

22

Is He a Painter or Not? 他是不是画家？

Learning Objectives

交际话题 Topic of conversation:

职业 Occupations
Zhíyè

基本句型 Sentence patterns:

他是医生。　　　他是记者吧？

他是不是画家？　我喜欢记者的工作。

New Words

1. 教师 jiàoshī　n. teacher
2. 司机 sījī　n. driver
3. 医生 yīshēng　n. doctor
4. 护士 hùshì　n. nurse
5. 科学家 kēxuéjiā　n. scientist
6. 记者 jìzhě　n. journalist
7. 工程师 gōngchéngshī　n. engineer
8. 工人 gōngrén　n. worker
9. 画家 huàjiā　n. painter
10. 工作 gōngzuò　n. occupation, job
11. 吧 ba　part. used at the end of the sentence to make a suggestion, express request or show agreement.

Text

Part I

本：这是我爸爸。
Běn: Zhè shì wǒ Bàba.

小雨：你爸爸是教师吗？
Xiǎoyǔ: Nǐ Bàba shì Jiàoshī ma?

本：不，他是医生。
Běn: Bù, tā shì yīshēng.

小雨：这是谁？是你哥哥吗？
Xiǎoyǔ: Zhè shì shuí? Shì nǐ gēge ma?

本：他是我哥哥。
Běn: Tā shì wǒ gēge.

小雨：你哥哥是不是画家？
Xiǎoyǔ: Nǐ gēge shì bú shì huàjiā?

本：他是画家。
Běn: Tā shì huàjiā.

小雨：这个人呢？是谁？
Xiǎoyǔ: Zhège rén ne? Shì shuí?

本：这是哥哥的朋友。
Běn: Zhè shì gēge de péngyou.

小雨：他是记者吧？
Xiǎoyǔ: Tā shì jìzhě ba?

本：你知道他？
Běn: Nǐ zhīdào tā?

小雨：知道，他很有名。
Xiǎoyǔ: Zhīdào, tā hěn yǒumíng.

Ben: This is my dad.
Xiaoyu: Is your dad a teacher?
Ben: No. He is a doctor.
Xiaoyu: Who is this? Is this your elder brother?
Ben: Yes. He is my elder brother.
Xiaoyu: Is he a painter or not?
Ben: He is a painter.
Xiaoyu: How about this? Who is this?
Ben: This is my elder brother's friend.
Xiaoyu: Is he a journalist?
Ben: Do you know him?
Xiaoyu: Yes, I do. He is very famous.

Learning Tip

Here is a useful sentence pattern to use if you want to develop your speaking, 一个是……一个是……。
This pattern is useful when talking about two people in one sentence, especially when talking about our family, their hobbies and their work.
For example: 我有两个哥哥，一个是医生，一个是司机。

大海： 你喜欢什么 工作?
Dàhǎi： Nǐ xǐhuan shénme gōngzuò?

京京： 我对很多 工作 有兴趣，你喜欢
Jīngjīng： Wǒ duì hěn duō gōngzuò yǒu xìngqù, nǐ xǐhuan

什么工作?
shénme gōngzuò?

大海： 我也对 很多 工作 有兴趣。教师、
Dàhǎi： Wǒ yě duì hěn duō gōngzuò yǒu xìngqù. Jiàoshī,

科学家、工程师，我都喜欢。
kēxuéjiā, gōngchéngshī, wǒ dōu xǐhuan.

京京： 我喜欢 工程师 的 工作。
Jīngjīng： Wǒ xǐhuan gōngchéngshī de gōngzuò.

Dahai: What job do you like?

Jingjing: I'm interested in many jobs. What job do you like?

Dahai: I'm also interested in lots of jobs.

Teacher, scientist, engineer, I like them all.

Jingjing: I like engineer.

Part II

他们的工作

这是我的家。我爸爸是教师，妈妈是护士。我有一个弟弟和一个姐姐，弟弟是中学生，姐姐是画家。我喜欢科学，对科学家的工作很有兴趣。

这是我的同学，他叫飞飞，他爸爸是工人，妈妈没有工作。他有两个哥哥，一个是司机，一个是电影演员。飞飞喜欢记者的工作。

Grammar Point

1. 吧 is used at the end of a sentence to express a polite request, make a suggestion, or show agreement. It is similar to 'aren't you' and 'isn't he'. It is also a useful word of expressing 'how about we...' or 'let's...'

e.g. 你爸爸是记者吧?
我们一起去图书馆吧。

Exercises

Listen 1　Number the following items in the order that they are played in the recording.

Listen 2　Listen to the recording and put a cross (X) in the correct box.

1) Jake is a ....

☐	teacher
☐	doctor
☐	student
☐	painter

2) Jake like the profession of ....

☐	student
☐	doctor
☐	teacher
☐	painter

3) Jake's brother is a ....

☐	student
☐	doctor
☐	teacher
☐	painter

4) .... is famous.

☐	Jake
☐	Jake's brother
☐	Jake's mother
☐	The speaker

Read 3　Read the sentence and match it with picture A or B.

A

B

他是不是医生？

你妹妹是不是演员？

她妈妈是教师吧？

你是记者吗？

她是科学家。

那个人不是工程师。

Read 4 Read the following paragraph and put a cross (X) next to the true statements.

　　我爸爸是医生，他喜欢医生的工作，我妹妹也喜欢。我不喜欢，医生的工作没意思。我对流行音乐有兴趣，我也喜欢电影演员的工作，流行音乐和表演的工作很有意思。

Example	My dad is a doctor.	×
	My dad likes his job.	
	I also like working as a doctor.	
	My sister doesn't like working as a doctor.	
	I find working as a doctor boring.	
	My sister likes pop music.	
	I find pop music boring.	
	I like working as an actor.	

Speak 5 Talk about the pictures in Chinese.

Speak **6** Role play. Tell your partner the professions of your family members and whether they like their jobs. Also ask your partner about what kind of job he/she is interested in.

e.g. 我爸爸是医生。他喜欢他的工作。
我妹妹是记者，她不喜欢她的工作。

你喜欢什么工作？/你对什么工作有兴趣？
我对老师的工作有兴趣。

Write **7** Complete the sentences with appropriate Chinese characters.

1）你妈妈是 ☐ ☐ 画家？

2）他爸爸是医生，☐ 妈妈也是。

3）开车的人是 ☐ ☐ 。

4）她妈妈是中学的 ☐ ☐ ，她有很多学生。

5）今天是周末，我哥哥没有 ☐ ☐ ，在家休息。

6）你是学生 ☐ ？　　(You are a student, aren't you?)

Write
8

Translate the sentences into English.

1) 你的朋友是一个有名的画家吧？我知道他。

....

2) 他姐姐是不是英国人？

....

3) 你对什么工作有兴趣？

....

4) 她有两个哥哥，一个是工程师，一个是记者。

....

Write
9

Translate the text below into Chinese.

Tiantian (天天) is my friend. He is a student. He is interested in music and performance. Tiantian and I went to a pop music concert together this weekend. Tiantian likes the profession of being an actor. It is interesting to be an actor.

....

....

....

Write 10 Practise Chinese characters.

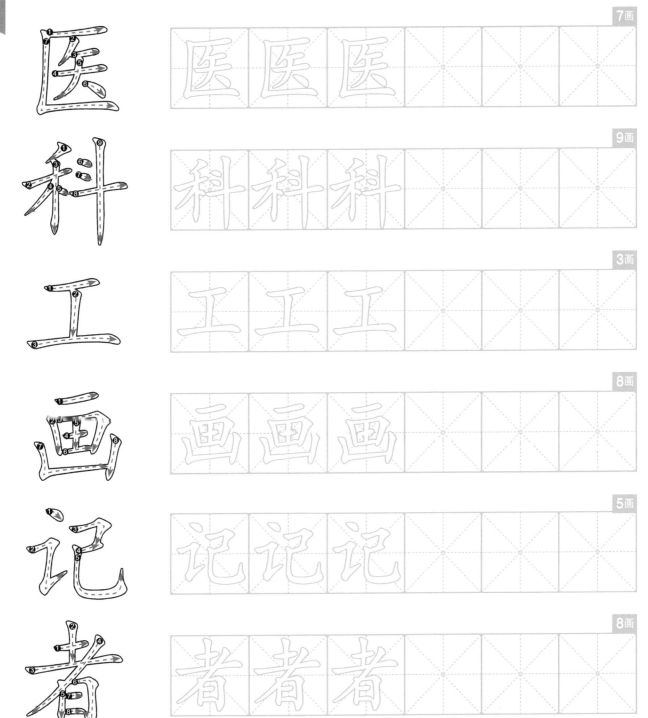

第二十三课 Lesson 23

I Want to Go to Shanghai 我想去上海

Learning Objectives

交际话题 Topic of conversation:

假期计划 Holiday Plans
Jiàqī jìhuà

基本句型 Sentence patterns:

(放假)多少天？　(放假)十四天。我想去法国。

New Words

1. 放 fàng　v. to put, to set free
2. 放假 fàng jià　to break up, to have a holiday
3. 假期 jiàqī　n. holiday, vacation
4. 暑假 shǔjià　n. summer holiday
5. 天 tiān　n. day
6. 旅行 lǚxíng　v. to travel
7. 高兴 gāoxìng　adj. happy
8. 想 xiǎng　v. to want; would like to
9. 一起 yìqǐ　adv. together

Text

Part I

爸爸： 这个星期我们开始放假。
Bàba: Zhège xīngqī wǒmen kāishǐ fàng jià.

妈妈： 放假多少天?
Māma: Fàng jià duōshao tiān?

爸爸： 十四天。
Bàba: Shísì tiān.

妈妈： 你想去旅行吗?
Māma: Nǐ xiǎng qù lǚxíng ma?

爸爸： 现在你和大卫都没有假期，我不去旅行。
Bàba: Xiànzài nǐ hé Dàwèi dōu méiyǒu jiàqī, wǒ bú qù lǚxíng.

妈妈： 七月大卫放暑假，我们三个人一起去旅行吧。
Māma: Qī yuè Dàwèi fàng shǔjià, wǒmen sān gè rén yìqǐ qù lǚxíng ba.

爸爸： 好! 大卫会很高兴。
Bàba: Hǎo! Dàwèi huì hěn gāoxìng.

Dad: We will be on holiday this week.
Mum: How long are you on holiday for?
Dad: Fourteen days.
Mum: Would you like to go travelling?
Dad: You and David don't have holidays now. I'm not going.
Mum: David will have his summer holiday in July. Let's travel at that time together.
Dad: Great! David will be very happy.

Learning Tip
Remember 一起 'together' must be used in front of verbs (actions). This is different from English. For example: 我们一起去旅行吧。

玛丽： 放暑假了，你想去哪儿?
Mǎlì: Fàng shǔjià le, nǐ xiǎng qù nǎr?

大卫： 我想去法国旅行。
Dàwèi: Wǒ xiǎng qù Fǎguó lǚxíng.

玛丽： 去多少天?
Mǎlì: Qù duōshao tiān?

Mary: It's summer holiday now.
    Where do you want to go?
David: I want to go to France.
Mary: How many days would you like to go?

大卫： 去一个星期。
Dàwèi：　Qù yí gè xīngqī.

玛丽： 你和谁去?
Mǎlì：　Nǐ hé shuí qù?

大卫： 和爸爸妈妈一起去。
Dàwèi：　Hé bàba māma yìqǐ qù.

玛丽： 坐飞机去吗?
Mǎlì：　Zuò fēijī qù ma?

大卫： 是，坐飞机去。
Dàwèi：　Shì, zuò fēijī qù.

David: A week.
Mary: Who are you going with?
David: With my parents.
Mary: Are you going by air?
David: Yes. By plane.

Learning Tip

要 and 想 have similar meanings when followed by a verb. It might help to think of 要 in this sense as meaning 'want to' and 想 as meaning 'would like to'. 想 feels less demanding and even polite. 要 is also used to indicate plans for the near future, much like "going to" in English.

Part II

放假了

　　放假了，假期没有课。我每天打篮球、上网、看电视、看电影，玩得很高兴。

　　假期我家去旅行。爸爸妈妈想开车去法国，在那儿玩六天。我的好朋友本也去旅行。他们家对中国北京很有兴趣，想坐飞机去那儿玩八天。

　　他们要去吃中国菜、看中国的表演、听中国的流行音乐。中国的流行音乐很好听。

8月15日

Grammar Point

1. 想 'would like to...' is a modal verb, which can be followed by another verb (action) to express willingness.

For example: 他们想去吃中国菜。
　　　　　　 我想坐飞机去上海。

Exercises

Listen 1   Listen to the recording and put a cross (X) in the correct boxes.

1)   ☐ I want to travel during the weekend.

     ☐ I want to travel during the holiday.

2)   ☐ Father doesn't have a summer vacation.

     ☐ Father doesn't have a job.

3)   ☐ We had a good time during the weekend.

     ☐ We had a good time during the summer vacation.

4)   ☐ There are 50 days in the summer holiday.

     ☐ There are 40 days in the summer holiday.

5)   ☐ This summer holiday is interesting.

     ☐ This summer holiday is not interesting.

Listen 2   Listen to the recording and answer the following questions in English.

1) How long is her holiday?

....

2) Who is she going to London with?

....

3) How long are they going to London for?

....

4) How are they getting there?

....

Read
3

Read the sentence and match it with picture A or B.

假期天气好不好？

她不放暑假。

我放假两天。

他们坐火车旅行。

她想去游泳。

我不想看电视。

Read
4 Read the following paragraph then use the words in the box to complete the translation. There are words that you will not need to use.

今天我们放假了。今天是晴天，天气很好，不冷也不热，外边没有风。上午我和朋友们打篮球，中午去吃中国菜，下午玩游戏，晚上看电视，今天的电视节目有足球比赛。在假期，我想每天都玩得高兴。

rainy   windy   sunny   hot   cold   not too cold or too hot   play football

play basketball   play tennis   have Chinese food   watch TV   watch movies

watch a football match   read books   play games

Today's weather is .... The temperature is .... I will ....

in the morning. I will .... in the afternoon. I will .... in the evening.

Speak
5 Talk about the pictures. How long are they going on holiday for and what would they like to do?

e.g. Peter 放假两天。 他想去开车旅行。

Speak 6 Role play. Tell your partner how long your summer holiday is and what you would like to do.

　　e.g. 我放暑假三十五天。　我想和爸爸妈妈一起去旅游。

Write 7 Complete the sentences with appropriate Chinese characters.

1）这个星期你们 ☐ 暑假了吗?

2）他不去旅行，他的爸爸妈妈没有 ☐ ☐ 。

3）你想怎么 ☐ ? 坐火车? 坐飞机?

4）我们放假两 ☐ ，你们放假多少 ☐ ?

5）今天晚上电视有好看的电影，我很 ☐ 看。

6）我 ☐ 去法国旅行。(would like to) 。

7） 放假了，我去中国 ☐ ☐ 。

8） 放假了，我想 ☐ 我哥哥 ☐ ☐ 去法国。 （together with...）

Write 8 Translate the sentences into English.

1） 我放暑假三十天。

....

2） 我们去上海玩十五天。

....

3） 我想和我朋友一起去法国旅行。

....

4） 我们坐火车去吧。

....

Write 9 Translate the following paragraph into Chinese.

> We started our holiday this week. I will be on holiday for two weeks. I would like to go to Hong Kong with my elder sister. Hong Kong's weather will be nice, it will be sunny. Hong Kong is hot. We are going there by plane next week.

....

....

....

Write
10
Practise Chinese characters.

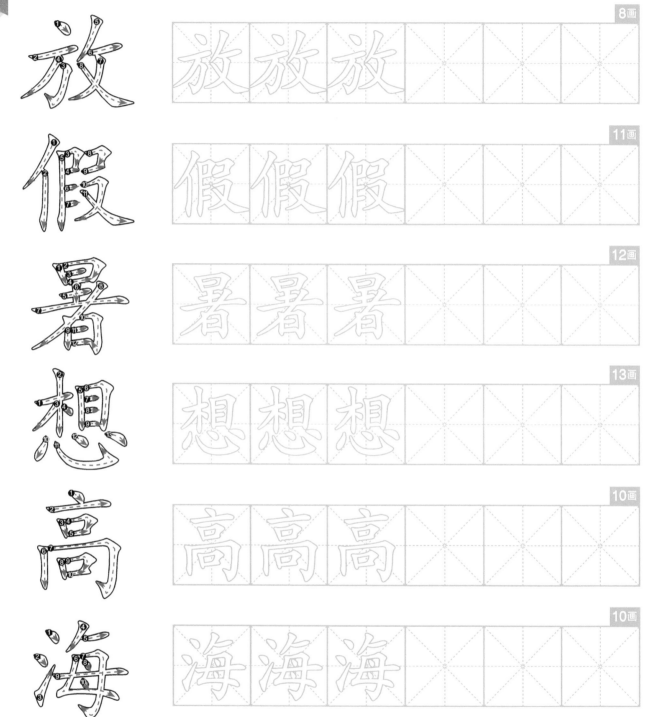

8画

11画

12画

13画

10画

10画

I'm Going to Be an Actress 我打算做演员 **24**

Learning Objectives

交际话题 Topic of conversation:

工作打算　Job Plans
Gōngzuò dǎsuàn

基本句型 Sentence patterns:

我打算做演员。　你唱歌唱得很好听。　先……再……

New Words

1. 做　zuò　**v.** to do, to become
2. 将来　jiānglái　**n.** future
3. 打算　dǎsuàn　**v./n.** to plan; plan
4. 唱歌　chàng gē　**v./n.** to sing; singing
5. 跳舞　tiào wǔ　**v./n.** to dance; dancing
6. 先　xiān　**adv.** firstly
7. 再　zài　**adv.** then
8. 然后　ránhòu　**adv.** and then, afterwards
9. 歌星　gēxīng　**n.** singer, pop star
10. 演唱会　yǎnchànghuì　**n.** concert

Text

Part I

京京： 你妈妈今天不在家吗？
Jīngjīng： Nǐ māma jīntiān bú zài jiā ma?

小雨： 她今天不休息，要工作。
Xiǎoyǔ： Tā jīntiān bù xiūxi, yào gōngzuò.

京京： 今天是周末，你妈妈也要工作吗？
Jīngjīng： Jīntiān shì zhōumò, nǐ māma yě yào gōngzuò ma?

小雨： 她是医生，常常没有周末。
Xiǎoyǔ： Tā shì yīshēng, chángcháng méiyǒu zhōumò.

将来我不想做医生，
Jiānglái wǒ bù xiǎng zuò yīshēng,

这个工作没意思。
zhège gōngzuò méi yìsi.

京京： 将来你打算做什么？
Jīngjīng： Jiānglái nǐ dǎsuàn zuò shénme?

小雨： 我打算做演员。
Xiǎoyǔ： Wǒ dǎsuàn zuò yǎnyuán.

京京： 是电影演员吗？
Jīngjīng： Shì diànyǐng yǎnyuán ma?

小雨： 是，我喜欢电影，对电影表演很有兴趣。
Xiǎoyǔ： Shì, wǒ xǐhuan diànyǐng, duì diànyǐng biǎoyǎn hěn yǒu xìngqù.

你呢？你打算做什么？
Nǐ ne? Nǐ dǎsuàn zuò shénme?

京京： 我喜欢唱歌、跳舞，将来我想做有名的歌星，
Jīngjīng： Wǒ xǐhuan chàng gē, tiào wǔ, jiānglái wǒ xiǎng zuò yǒumíng de gēxīng,

每个人都知道我。
měi gè rén dōu zhīdào wǒ.

小雨： 是，你唱歌唱得很好听，跳舞也跳得很好看。
Xiǎoyǔ： Shì, nǐ chàng gē chàng de hěn hǎotīng, tiào wǔ yě tiào de hěn hǎokàn.

Jingjing: Isn't your mother at home?

Xiaoyu: No, she isn't. She has to work.

Jingjing: Today is the weekend. Does she still need to work?

Xiaoyu: She's a doctor. She has to work during the weekend.
I don't want to be a doctor in the future. This job is boring.

Jingjing: What are you planning to do in the future?

Xiaoyu: I'm going to be an actress.

Jingjing: A movie actress?

Xiaoyu: Yes. I like movies. I'm very interested in film performance.
How about you? What are you going to do?

Jingjing: I like singing and dancing. I want to be a famous singer in the future.
Everyone will know me then.

Xiaoyu: Yes. You can both sing and dance very well.

Part II

我想做一个记者

我叫丽丽，我现在是一个中学生。我对新闻节目很有兴趣，将来我想做一个记者，做电视新闻。我的姐姐喜欢音乐，她对古典音乐很有兴趣，将来想在演唱会上表演。我的妹妹喜欢看书，将来她想做一个科学家。我的哥哥喜欢旅行和运动，也常常上网。现在我们都不知道将来会做什么，先做学生，再做将来的打算。

Grammar Point

1. Talking about the future is much easier in Chinese. There's no need to change the form of the verb or add anything to it. Simply use a time phrase that indicates the future, like 将来，明天，下个星期, and/or use verbs such as 想，要，打算.
For example:
你将来打算做什么？我打算做演员。
你下个星期放假想去哪儿？我想去中国旅行。

2. 先……，再/然后……is a pattern used for sequencing events, much like 'First ...., then ....' in English.
Use the following pattern:
先 + verb 1 (action 1) + 再/然后 + verb 2 (action 2)
e.g.哥哥打算先踢足球，再/然后打篮球。
我想先吃面条，再/然后吃苹果。

Exercises

Listen 1 Listen to the recording and put a cross (X) in the correct boxes.

1) ☐ I plan to be a doctor in the future.

☐ I plan to be an actor in the future.

2) ☐ This actor is very famous.

☐ This singer is very famous.

3) ☐ She sings very well.

☐ She swims very well.

4) ☐ You have a rest first and then have dinner.

☐ You have dinner and then have a rest.

5) ☐ She dances very well.

☐ She is a good actress.

Listen 2 Listen to the recording and complete the sentences by choosing a word or words from the box. There are words that you will not need to use.

painter   journalist   singer   actress   classical music   dancing   pop music   acting

morning   afternoon   evening   play games   read books   have a meal   go to visit Lily

go to visit Lily's sister   go to Lily's sister's concert

Lily's sister is a famous .... She is very interested in .... There is no

class this .... My friends and I will first .... , then ....

Read 3 Read the sentence and match it with picture A or B.

将来你打算做教师吗?

现在我们先休息，下午再比赛。

周末你有什么打算？

我不想先开始。

我想先去打球，然后去吃饭。

他不打算坐火车旅行。

Read 4 Read the paragraph and put a cross (X) in the correct box for each question.

今天我们班上中文课，很多同学说（speak）了他们将来的打算，
玛丽打算做法语教师，本想做游泳运动员。想做医生的同学最多，最
不想做的工作是工程师。

1) Mary plans to become a . . . .

☐	engineer
☐	French teacher
☐	swimming athlete
☐	doctor

2) Ben would like to become a . . . .

☐	engineer
☐	French teacher
☐	swimming athlete
☐	doctor

3) The most popular job is . . . .

☐	engineer
☐	French teacher
☐	swimming athlete
☐	doctor

4) The least popular job is . . . .

☐	engineer
☐	French teacher
☐	swimming athlete
☐	doctor

Speak 5 Talk about the pictures. Describe to your partner what each of the characters are interested in and what they plan to do in the future.

e.g. 京京对看书有兴趣。她打算做科学家。

我弟弟
My younger brother

我姐姐
My elder sister

Speak 6 Role play. Tell your partner about your interests and what you would like to become in the future.

e.g. 我最喜欢表演，将来我想做演员。

Write 7 Complete the sentences with appropriate Chinese characters.

1）我叫 .... ，是 .... 国人。

2）我的爱好是 .... 。我也喜欢 .... 。

3）我常常 .... 。

4）我对 .... 有兴趣。

5）我喜欢 .... 。

6）我打算先 .... ，再 .... 。

Write 8

Translate the sentences into English.

1）将来你想做什么？

....

2）我妹妹跳舞跳得很好。

....

3）这个周末我们打算去看中国电影。

....

4）今天晚上我们先吃中国面条，然后喝英国茶。

....

Write 9

Translate the following paragraph into Chinese.

My elder sister likes sports. She often runs, and plays football and tennis together with her friends. She likes playing tennis the most. She plays tennis very well. She plans to be a tennis player. Today is Sunday, she has no class. She went to the stadium to play tennis.

....

....

....

....

Write
10
Practise Chinese characters.

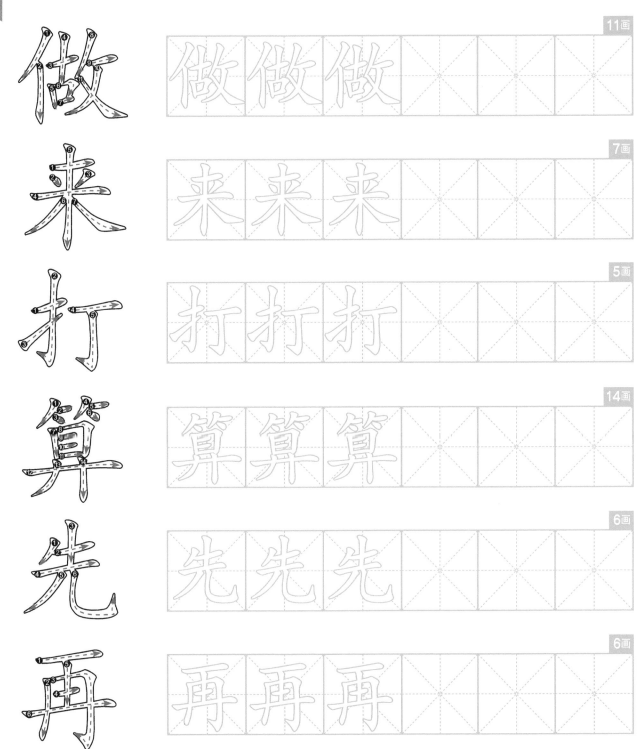

11画

做 做 做

7画

来 来 来

5画

打 打 打

14画

算 算 算

6画

先 先 先

6画

再 再 再

Dream jobs of Chinese young generation

In 2017, there were more that 400 million young adults in China. That is a third of China's population, and it is equal to the whole working population of the US and Western Europe combined. This generation of Chinese is different from those that came before it. This generation of young adults are already exerting significant influence in modern culture and attitudes towards family, relationships and work.

In 2017, US-based networking website, LinkedIn, did an interesting survey into the dream jobs of China's young generation. For Chinese men born after 1980, the dream is to become a civil servant; and for women, it is to become a teacher. The survey also found that, after civil service, Chinese men dreamed of being scientists, policemen, and teachers. For women, the second choices were medical worker, artist, public servant and designer.

However, top jobs for respondents born after 1990 were much more different. Nearly half responded that they want to be a corporate manager, pilot, flight attendant, movie director or photographer.

This survey shows that young people have more variety in their dream jobs. People born after 1980 are looking for stable work with a traditionally good social standing. However, with access to information, social values have become increasingly diversified. Many young people now make decisions based on their interests rather than choosing occupations that were highly recognised in the traditional sense.

第八单元小结　Unit Eight　Summary

Talking about professions

我是医生。 I am a doctor. 她不是演员。 She is not an actor.	Someone + （不）是 + profession
你是演员吗? 你是不是演员? Are you an actor?	Someone + 是 + profession + 吗? Someone + 是不是 + profession?
你是演员吧? You are an actor, aren't you?	Someone + 是 + profession + 吧? (seeking confirmation)

Talking about holidays

放暑假了。 Summer holiday has started	New Situation + 了 （indicates change of situation）
放假多少天? How long are you on holiday for 放假十四天。 I am on holiday for 14 days.	Topic + comment 放假 + 多少 + 天? 放假 + number + 天。
去上海多少天? How long are you going to Shanghai for? 去上海六天。 I am going to Shanghai for 6 days.	Topic + comment Activity + 多少 + 天? Activity + number + 天。
一起去旅行 go travelling together	一起 + verb （action）
我们一起去旅行吧。 Let us go traveling together.	Statement + 吧。（making suggestion）
你和谁一起去? Who are you going with? 我和爸爸妈妈一起去。 I am going with my mum and dad.	someone + 和 + someone else + 一起 + verb (action)

第八单元小结　Unit Eight　Summary

Talking about plans

你想去哪儿？ Where would you like to go? 我想去法国。 I would like to go to France.	someone + 想 + verb (action) + something/somewhere
你打算做什么？ What are you planning to do? 我打算做演员。 I am planning to become an actor.	someone + 打算 + verb （action） + something/someone
先踢足球，然后打篮球 play football first, then play basketball 先做学生，再做将来的打算 study first, then make plans for the future	先 + verb 1 (action 1) + 再/然后 + verb 2 (action 2)

A. Chinese-English Vocabulary List

生字词	拼音	词性	英文
爱好	àihào	n.	hobby
吧	ba	part.	used at the end of the sentence to make a suggestion, express request or show agreement
八	bā	num.	eight
爸爸	bàba	n.	father
百	bǎi	num.	hundred
半	bàn	num.	half
班	bān	n.	class
北京	Běijīng	n.	Beijing
本	běn	m.w.	a measure word for books
表演	biǎoyǎn	n.	performance
比赛	bǐsài	n.	match, competition
不	bù	adv.	not
茶	chá	n.	tea
常常	chángcháng	adv.	often
唱歌	chàng gē	v./n.	to sing; singing
吃	chī	v.	to eat
打	dǎ	v.	to hit, to play (other ball games than football)
打算	dǎsuàn	v. / n.	to plan; plan
大	dà	adj.	big
的	de	part.	a structual particle
得	de	part.	a structual particle
等	děng	v.	to wait for
点	diǎn	m.w.	o'clock
电视	diànshì	n.	TV (programme)
电视机	diànshìjī	n.	TV set
电影	diànyǐng	n.	film, movie
电子游戏	diànzǐ yóuxì	n.	computer games
弟弟	dìdi	n.	younger brother
都	dōu	adv.	both, all
读	dú	v.	to read
对	duì	prep.	to, for
多	duō	adj.	many, how (+adj.)
多少	duōshao	pron.	how many/much
二	èr	num.	two
二十	èrshí	num.	twenty
二十五	èrshíwǔ	num.	twenty-five
法国	Fǎguó	n.	France

生字词	拼音	词性	英文
法文	Fǎwén	n.	French
饭	fàn	n.	meal
放	fàng	v.	to put, to set free
放假	fàng jià	v.	to break up, to have a holiday
房间	fángjiān	n.	room
飞机	fēijī	n.	plane
飞机场	fēijīchǎng	n.	airport
分	fēn	m.w.	minute
风	fēng	n.	wind
粉红(色)	fěnhóng(sè)	adj.	pink
高兴	gāoxìng	adj.	happy
个	gè	m.w.	a measure word
哥哥	gēge	n.	elder brother
歌星	gēxīng	n.	singer, pop star
工程师	gōngchéngshī	n.	engineer
公共汽车	gōnggòng qìchē	n.	bus
工人	gōngrén	n.	worker
工作	gōngzuò	n.	occupation, job
狗	gǒu	n.	dog
古典	gǔdiǎn	adj.	classical
果汁	guǒzhī	n.	juice
海鲜	hǎixiān	n.	seafood
好	hǎo	adj.	good, fine
号/日	hào/rì	n.	date
好听	hǎotīng	adj.	pleasing to the ear
和	hé	conj.	and, with
喝	hē	v.	to drink
很	hěn	adv.	very
红(色)	hóng(sè)	adj.	red
后边	hòubian	n.	back side; behind
画家	huàjiā	n.	painter
黄(色)	huáng(sè)	adj.	yellow
回来	huílái	v.	to return, to come back
会	huì	v.	can; to be able to; to have the skill to
火车	huǒchē	n.	train
火车站	huǒchēzhàn	n.	railway station
护士	hùshì	n.	nurse
鸡蛋	jīdàn	n.	egg

生字词	拼音	词性	英文
几	jǐ	pron.	how many
记者	jìzhě	n.	journalist
家	jiā	n.	home, family
假期	jiàqī	n.	holiday, vacation
见	jiàn	v.	to see
将来	jiānglái	n.	future
叫	jiào	v.	to call
教室	jiàoshì	n.	classroom
教师	jiàoshī	n.	teacher
节目	jiémù	n.	programme
姐姐	jiějie	n.	elder sister
今天	jīntiān	n.	today
九	jiǔ	num.	nine
咖啡	kāfēi	n.	coffee
开(车)	kāi(chē)	v.	to drive
开始	kāishǐ	v.	to begin
看	kàn	v.	to watch, to read
看书	kàn shū	v.	to read books
课	kè	n.	class
刻	kè	m.w.	quarter
科学家	kēxuéjiā	n.	scientist
口	kǒu	m.w./n.	measure word used when addressing the entire number of people in a family; mouth
快	kuài	adj.	fast, quick
篮球	lánqiú	n.	basketball
老师	lǎoshī	n.	teacher
了	le	part.	used after verbs (action words) to indicate an action is completed
冷	lěng	adj.	cold
两	liǎng	num.	two (before measure word)
零	líng	num.	zero
流行	liúxíng	adj.	popular
六	liù	num.	six
绿(色)	lǜ(sè)	adj.	green
伦敦	Lúndūn	n.	London
旅行	lǚxíng	v.	to travel
吗	ma	part.	used for 'Yes/No' questions
妈妈	māma	n.	mother
猫	māo	n.	cat

生字词	拼音	词性	英文
没	méi	adv.	not, no
没意思	méi yìsi	adj.	boring
每	měi	pron.	every
美国	Měiguó	n.	USA
美洲	Měizhōu	n.	America
妹妹	mèimei	n.	younger sister
米饭	mǐfàn	n.	rice
面包	miànbāo	n.	bread
面条	miàntiáo	n.	noodles
明天	míngtiān	n.	tomorrow
那	nà	pron.	that
哪	nǎ	pron.	which
奶奶	nǎinai	n.	grandmother
男	nán	adj.	male
男（学）生	nán(xué)sheng	n.	male student
哪儿	nǎr	pron.	where
呢	ne	part.	interrogative word
你	nǐ	pron.	you (singular)
你们	nǐmen	pron.	you (plural)
您	nín	pron.	the respectful form of 你 (singular)
牛奶	niúnǎi	n.	milk
牛肉	niúròu	n.	beef
女	nǚ	adj.	female
女（学）生	nǚ(xué)sheng	n.	female student
欧洲	Ōuzhōu	n.	Europe
旁边	pángbiān	n.	the side, next to
跑	pǎo	v.	to run
跑步	pǎobù	v. / n.	to run; jogging
朋友	péngyou	n.	friend
苹果	píngguǒ	n.	apple
乒乓球	pīngpāngqiú	n.	table tennis, ping-pong
七	qī	num.	seven
骑	qí	v.	to ride
前边	qiánbian	n./prep.	the front; in front of
汽车	qìchē	n.	vehicles in general
汽车站	qìchēzhàn	n.	bus station
青菜	qīngcài	n.	green vegetable
晴天	qíngtiān	n.	sunny day

生字词	拼音	词性	英文
请问	qǐngwèn		Excuse me
汽水	qìshuǐ	n.	soft drink
去	qù	v.	to go
然后	rán hòu	adv.	and then, afterwards
热	rè	adj.	hot
人	rén	n.	people
上	shàng	n.	up, top
上课	shàng kè		go to class
上海	Shànghǎi	n.	Shanghai
上网	shàng wǎng		to surf the Internet
上午	shàngwǔ	n.	morning
什么	shénme	pron.	what
生日	shēngri	n.	birthday
十	shí	num.	ten
是	shì	v.	to be (e.g. am; is; are)
书	shū	n.	book
蔬菜	shūcài	n.	vegetable
谁	shuí/shéi	pron.	who
水	shuǐ	n.	water
水果	shuǐguǒ	n.	fruit
暑假	shǔjià	n.	summer holiday
三	sān	num.	three
司机	sījī	n.	driver
四	sì	num.	four
他	tā	pron.	he, him
她	tā	pron.	she, her
台湾	Táiwān	n.	Taiwan
他们	tāmen	pron.	they, them
体育馆	tǐyùguǎn	n.	gymnasium, stadium
天	tiān	n.	day
天气	tiānqì	n.	weather
跳舞	tiào wǔ	v. / n.	to dance; dancing
踢	tī	v.	to kick, to play (football)
听	tīng	v.	to listen
同学	tóngxué	n.	classmate
图书馆	túshūguǎn	n.	library
外边	wàibiān	n.	outside
玩	wán	v.	to play (games)

生字词	拼音	词性	英文
往	wǎng	prep.	toward
网球	wǎngqiú	n.	tennis
晚上	wǎnshang	n.	evening
我	wǒ	n.	I, me
我们	wǒmen	pron.	we, us
五	wǔ	num.	five
喜欢	xǐhuan	v.	to like
下	xià	n.	down, below
下课	xià kè		finish class
下午	xiàwǔ	n.	afternoon
下雪	xià xuě	v.	to snow
下雨	xià yǔ	v.	to rain
先	xiān	adv.	firstly
现在	xiànzài	n.	now
香港	Xiānggǎng	n.	Hong Kong
想	xiǎng	v.	to want; would like to
小	xiǎo	adj.	small, little
谢谢	xièxie	v.	thank you
星期三	xīngqīsān	n.	Wednesday
星期四	xīngqīsì	n.	Thursday
兴趣	xìngqù	n.	interest
新闻	xīnwén	n.	news
休息	xiūxi	v.	to rest
雪	xuě	n.	snow
学生	xuésheng	n.	student
演唱会	yǎnchànghuì	n.	concert
演员	yǎnyuán	n.	actor/actress
要	yào	v.	to want
亚洲	Yàzhōu	n.	Asia
也	yě	adv.	also, too
爷爷	yéye	n.	grandfather
一	yī	num.	one
英国	Yīngguó	n.	UK, Britain
音乐	yīnyuè	n.	music
音乐会	yīnyuèhuì	n.	concert
一起	yìqǐ	adv.	together
医生	yīshēng	n.	doctor
游	yóu	v.	to swim

生字词	拼音	词性	英文
有	yǒu	v.	to have (indicates ownership or existence)
有意思	yǒu yìsi	adj.	interesting
右边	yòubian	n.	right side; the right
有名	yǒumíng	adj.	famous
游泳	yóuyǒng	v./n.	to swim; swimming
鱼	yú	n.	fish
雨	yǔ	n.	rain
预报	yùbào	n.	(weather) forecast
月	yuè	n.	month
运动	yùndòng	n.	sport, athletics
运动场	yùndòngchǎng	n.	sports ground, athletic ground
在	zài	v.	to be in, to be at
再	zài	adv.	then
早饭	zǎofàn	n.	breakfast
早上	zǎoshang	n.	morning
怎么	zěnme	adv.	how
怎么样	zěnmeyàng		what about
这	zhè	pron.	this
(正)在	(zhèng)zài	adv.	be doing sth.
只	zhī	m.w.	a measure word for certain animals, e.g., cat, dog, bird, etc.
知道	zhīdào	v.	to know
中	zhōng	n.	middle
中国	Zhōngguó	n.	China
中文	Zhōngwén	n.	Chinese
中午	zhōngwǔ	n.	noon
中学生	zhōngxuéshēng	n.	middle school student
周末	zhōumò	n.	weekend
自行车/单车	zìxíngchē/dānchē	n.	bike, bicycle
走	zǒu	v.	to walk, to go to somewhere
足球	zúqiú	n.	football, soccer
最	zuì	adv.	most
左边	zuǒbian	n.	left side; the left
坐	zuò	v.	to take or to travel by (a vehicle)
做	zuò	v.	to do, to become

B. **English-Chinese Vocabulary List**

英文	生字词	拼音	词性
a measure word	个	gè	m.w.
a measure word for books	本	běn	m.w.
a measure word for certain animals	只	zhī	m.w.
a structual particle	的	de	part.
a structual particle	得	de	part.
actor/actress	演员	yǎnyuán	n.
afternoon	下午	xiàwǔ	n.
airport	飞机场	fēijīchǎng	n.
also, too	也	yě	adv.
America	美洲	Měizhōu	n.
and	和	hé	conj.
and then, afterwards	然后	rán hòu	adv.
apple	苹果	píngguǒ	n.
Asia	亚洲	Yàzhōu	n.
back side; behind	后边	hòubian	n.
basketball	篮球	lánqiú	n.
be doing sth.	正在	zhèngzài	adv.
beef	牛肉	niúròu	n.
Beijing	北京	Běijīng	n.
big	大	dà	adj.
bike, bicycle	自行车/单车	zìxíngchē/dānchē	n.
birthday	生日	shēngri	n.
book	书	shū	n.
boring	没意思	méi yìsi	adj.
both, all	都	dōu	adv.
bread	面包	miànbāo	n.
breakfast	早饭	zǎofàn	n.
bus	公共汽车	gōnggòng qìchē	n.
can; to be able to; to have the skill to	会	huì	v.
car	汽车	qìchē	n.
cat	猫	māo	n.
China	中国	Zhōngguó	n.
Chinese	中文	Zhōngwén	n.
class	班	bān	n.
class	课	kè	n.
classical	古典	gǔdiǎn	adj.

英文	生字词	拼音	词性
classmate	同学	tóngxué	n.
classroom	教室	jiàoshì	n.
coffee	咖啡	kāfēi	n.
cold	冷	lěng	adj.
computer games	电子游戏	diànzyóuxì	n.
concert	演唱会	yǎnchànghuì	n.
concert	音乐会	yīnyuèhuì	n.
date	号／日	hào/rì	n.
day	天	tiān	n.
doctor	医生	yīshēng	n.
dog	狗	gǒu	n.
down, below	下	xià	n.
driver	司机	sījī	n.
eight	八	bā	num.
egg	鸡蛋	jīdàn	n.
elder brother	哥哥	gēge	n.
elder sister	姐姐	jiějie	n.
engineer	工程师	gōngchéngshī	n.
Europe	欧洲	Ōuzhōu	n.
evening	晚上	wǎnshang	n.
every	每	měi	pron.
Excuse me	请问	qǐngwèn	
famous	有名	yǒumíng	adj.
fast, quick	快	kuài	adj.
father	爸爸	bàba	n.
female	女	nǚ	adj.
female student	女（学）生	nǚ(xué)sheng	n.
film, movie	电影	diànyǐng	n.
firstly	先	xiān	adv.
fish	鱼	yú	n.
five	五	wǔ	num.
football, soccer	足球	zúqiú	n.
four	四	sì	num.
(weather) forecast	预报	yùbào	n.
France	法国	Fǎguó	n.
French	法文	Fǎwén	n.
friend	朋友	péngyou	n.
fruit	水果	shuǐguǒ	n.

英文	生字词	拼音	词性
future	将来	jiānglái	n.
go to class	上课	shàng kè	
good, fine	好	hǎo	adj.
grandfather	爷爷	yéye	n.
grandmother	奶奶	nǎinai	n.
green	绿(色)	lǜ(sè)	adj.
green vegetable	青菜	qīngcài	n.
gymnasium, stadium	体育馆	tǐyùguǎn	n.
half	半	bàn	num.
happy	高兴	gāoxìng	adj.
he; him	他	tā	pron.
hobby	爱好	àihào	n.
holiday, vacation	假期	jiàqī	n.
home, family	家	jiā	n.
Hong Kong	香港	Xiānggǎng	n.
hot	热	rè	adj.
how	怎么	zěnme	adv.
how many	几	jǐ	prop.
how many/much	多少	duōshao	pron.
hundred	百	bǎi	num.
I, me	我	wǒ	pron.
interest	兴趣	xìngqù	n.
interesting	有意思	yǒu yìsi	adj.
interrogative word	呢	ne	part.
interrogative word	吗	ma	part.
journalist	记者	jìzhě	n.
juice	果汁	guǒzhī	n.
left side; the left	左边	zuǒbian	n.
library	图书馆	túshūguǎn	n.
London	伦敦	Lúndūn	n.
male	男	nán	adj.
male student	男(学)生	nán(xué)sheng	n.
many, how (+adj.)	多	duō	adj.
match, competition	比赛	bǐsài	n.
meal	饭	fàn	n.
measure word used when addressing the entire number of people in a family; mouth	口	kǒu	m.w./n.
middle	中	zhōng	n.

英文	生字词	拼音	词性
middle school student	中学生	zhōngxuéshēng	n.
milk	牛奶	niúnǎi	n.
minute	分	fēn	m.w.
month	月	yuè	n.
morning	上午	shàngwǔ	n.
morning	早上	zǎoshang	n.
most	最	zuì	adv.
mother	妈妈	māma	n.
music	音乐	yīnyuè	n.
news	新闻	xīnwén	n.
next to	旁边	pángbiān	n.
nine	九	jiǔ	num.
noodles	面条	miàntiáo	n.
noon	中午	zhōngwǔ	n.
not	不	bù	adv.
not, no	没	méi	adv.
now	现在	xiànzài	n.
nurse	护士	hùshì	n.
occupation, job	工作	gōngzuò	n.
o'clock	点	diǎn	m.w.
often	常常	chángcháng	adv.
one	一	yī	num.
outside	外边	wàibian	n.
painter	画家	huàjiā	n.
people	人	rén	n.
performance	表演	biǎoyǎn	n.
pink	粉红(色)	fěnhóng(sè)	adj.
plane	飞机	fēijī	n.
pleasing to the ear	好听	hǎotīng	adj.
popular	流行	liúxíng	adj.
programme	节目	jiémù	n.
quarter	刻	kè	m.w.
railway station	火车站	huǒchēzhàn	n.
rain	雨	yǔ	n.
red	红(色)	hóng(sè)	adj.
rice	米饭	mǐfàn	n.
right side; the right	右边	yòubian	n.
room	房间	fángjiān	n.

英文	生字词	拼音	词性
scientist	科学家	kēxuéjiā	n.
seafood	海鲜	hǎixiān	n.
seven	七	qī	num.
six	六	liù	num.
Shanghai	上海	Shànghǎi	n.
she; her	她	tā	pron.
singer, pop star	歌星	gēxīng	n.
small, little	小	xiǎo	adj.
snow	雪	xuě	n.
soft drink	汽水	qìshuǐ	n.
sport, athletics	运动	yùndòng	n.
sports ground, athletic ground	运动场	yùndòngchǎng	n.
student	学生	xuésheng	n.
summer holiday	暑假	shǔjià	n.
sunny day	晴天	qíngtiān	n.
table tennis; ping-pong	乒乓球	pīngpāngqiú	n.
Taiwan	台湾	Táiwān	n.
tea	茶	chá	n.
teacher	教师	jiàoshī	n.
teacher	老师	lǎoshī	n.
ten	十	shí	num.
tennis	网球	wǎngqiú	n.
thank you	谢谢	xièxie	v.
that	那	nà	pron.
the front; in front of	前边	qiánbian	n./prep.
then	再	zài	adv.
they, them	他们	tāmen	pron.
this	这	zhè	pron.
three	三	sān	num.
Thursday	星期四	xīngqīsì	n.
to	对	duì	prep.
to be (e.g. am; is; are)	是	shì	v.
to be in; to be at	在	zài	v.
to begin	开始	kāishǐ	v.
to break up, to have a holiday	放假	fàng jià	
to call	叫	jiào	v.
to dance; dancing	跳舞	tiàowǔ	
to do, to become	做	zuò	v.

英文	生字词	拼音	词性
to drink	喝	hē	v.
to drive	开(车)	kāi(chē)	v.
to eat	吃	chī	v.
to finish class	下课	xià kè	
to go	去	qù	v.
to kick, to play (football)	踢	tī	v.
to have (indicates ownership or existence)	有	yǒu	v.
to know	知道	zhīdào	v.
to like	喜欢	xǐhuan	v.
to listen	听	tīng	v.
to plan; plan	打算	dǎsuàn	v. / n.
to play (games)	玩	wán	v.
to play (other ball games than football), to hit	打	dǎ	v.
to put, to set free	放	fàng	v.
to rain	下雨	xià yǔ	v.
to read	读书	dú shū	v.
to read books	看书	kàn shū	v.
to rest	休息	xiūxi	v.
to return, to come back	回来	huí lái	v.
to ride	骑	qí	v.
to run	跑	pǎo	v.
to run; jogging	跑步	pǎobù	v. / n.
to see	见	jiàn	v.
to sing; singing	唱歌	chànggē	v./n.
to snow	下雪	xià xuě	v.
to surf the Internet	上网	shàng wǎng	
to swim	游	yóu	v.
to swim; swimming	游泳	yóuyǒng	v./n.
to take or to travel by (a vehicle)	坐	zuò	v.
to travel	旅行	lǚxíng	v.
to wait for	等	děng	v.
to walk, to go to somewhere	走	zǒu	v.
to want; would like to	想	xiǎng	v.
to watch	看	kàn	v.
today	今天	jīntiān	n.
together	一起	yìqǐ	adv.
tomorrow	明天	míngtiān	n.
toward	往	wǎng	prep.

英文	生字词	拼音	词性
train	火车	huǒchē	n.
TV (programme)	电视	diànshì	n.
TV set	电视机	diànshìjī	n.
twenty	二十	èrshí	num.
twenty-five	二十五	èrshíwǔ	num.
two	二	èr	num.
two (before measure word)	两	liǎng	num.
USA	美国	Měiguó	n.
UK; Britain	英国	Yīngguó	n.
up, top	上	shàng	n.
used at the end of the sentence to make a suggestion, express request or show agreement	吧	ba	part.
used after verbs (action words) to indicate an action is completed	了	le	part.
vegetable	蔬菜	shūcài	n.
vehicles in general	汽车	qìchē	n.
very	很	hěn	adv.
water	水	shuǐ	n.
we, us	我们	wǒmen	pron.
weather	天气	tiānqì	n.
Wednesday	星期三	xīngqīsān	n.
weekend	周末	zhōumò	n.
what	什么	shénme	pron.
what about	怎么样	zěnmeyàng	
where	哪儿	nǎr	pron.
which	哪	nǎ	prep.
who	谁	shuí/shéi	pron.
wind	风	fēng	n.
worker	工人	gōngrén	n.
yellow	黄(色)	huáng(sè)	adj.
you (singular)	你	nǐ	pron.
you (plural)	你们	nǐmen	pron.
you (respectful form of 你)	您	nín	pron.
younger brother	弟弟	dìdi	n.
younger sister	妹妹	mèimei	n.
zero	零	líng	num.